D0317348

OFFICE FOR STANDARDS
IN EDUCATION

Guidance on the Inspection of SECONDARY SCHOOLS

Issued by Her Majesty's Chief Inspector of Schools in England

London: HMSO

INTRODUCTION

This *Handbook* is published by Her Majesty's Chief Inspector of Schools (HMCI) for inspectors of secondary and middle-deemed-secondary schools and pupil referral units (PRUs) for secondary age pupils. It includes:

■ the *OFSTED Framework* for the inspection of schools under Section 9 of the Education (Schools) Act 1992; and

■ guidance on the conduct of inspections and on inspecting schools to the schedule for inspection in the *Framework*.

Part I consists of the **inspection requirements** which form part of the *Framework*. It sets out the principles on which inspections are based and the general requirements which are to be met by registered inspectors.

Part II provides **guidance on conducting inspections** in line with the inspection requirements. It focuses in particular on the role of registered inspectors leading inspections and outlines what they need to do before, during and after the inspection, *but it is important that all inspectors are aware of the contents*:

■ the specific requirements for evaluating and reporting on the work of the school and the standards achieved by pupils; and

■ the criteria which form the basis for arriving at judgements.

The guidance seeks to establish the main focus of inspection, provides advice on using the criteria and forming judgements in relation to each aspect of the schedule, and indicates key sources of evidence.

Part III of the *Handbook* also includes general guidance on the inspection of subjects and areas of learning of the curriculum.

Guidance in the *Handbook* is intended to help ensure that the inspection process is of the highest quality and that judgements about a school are both fair and rigorous. A good inspection is one where:

■ judgements about the educational standards achieved by the school and the strengths and weaknesses in teaching and the other aspects inspected are objective, reliable and secure;

■ the main findings and the key issues for action to raise educational standards achieved by pupils in the school are clearly identified and reported to the school;

and, through the conduct of the inspection:

■ inspectors establish an effective working relationship with the school based on professionalism, sensitivity, and an understanding of the school's concerns and its circumstances;

Office for Standards in Education
Alexandra House
29-33 Kingsway
London WC2B 6SE

© Crown copyright 1995
Applications for reproduction should be made to HMSO's Copyright Unit
Second impression 1996

ISBN 0 11 350067 X

CONTENTS

- the process is well planned and effectively managed;

- there are good communications with the school which lead to a clear and shared understanding of what is involved at each stage;

- inspectors readily explore issues with staff through professional dialogue;

- judgements are made on the basis of the proper collection of the required evidence, through the application of appropriate criteria and the exercise of professional expertise; and

- feedback to the school and the governing body, both orally and in writing, is clear and comprehensible.

Inspectors should leave the staff and governors feeling that they have gained from the contact with members of the team, as well as recognising the thoroughness of the evidence base and understanding and respecting the judgements which emerge. Those involved in running the school should feel that the inspection has provided a valuable component of their strategy for improvement.

PART I

THE OFSTED FRAMEWORK: INSPECTION REQUIREMENTS

THE PURPOSE OF INSPECTION

1 The purpose of inspection is to identify strengths and weaknesses so that schools may improve the quality of education they provide and raise the educational standards achieved by their pupils. The published report and summary report provide information for parents and the local community about the quality and standards of the school, consistent with the requirements of the *Parent's Charter*. The inspection process, feedback and reports give direction to the school's strategy for planning, review and improvement by providing rigorous external evaluation and identifying key issues for action. Inspection findings also provide a basis for the national evaluation of schools and the annual report of Her Majesty's Chief Inspector of Schools in England (HMCI).

STATUTORY BASIS FOR INSPECTIONS BY REGISTERED INSPECTORS

2 Inspection of a school[1] under Section 9 of the Education (Schools) Act 1992 (the 1992 Act) requires inspectors to report on:

the quality of the education provided by the school;

the educational standards achieved in the school;

whether the financial resources made available to the school are managed efficiently; and

the spiritual, moral, social and cultural development of pupils at the school.

3 HMCI requires all registered inspectors to comply with the *OFSTED Framework* (the *Framework*) as a condition of registration, subject to any amendment issued by HMCI or to the contract specification for an individual inspection. Registered inspectors must be familiar with their statutory duties[2].

4 The *Framework* forms the basis for assuring the standard of inspections. Judgements must be secured by appropriate evidence, and the consistent use of evaluation criteria, and informed by quantitative indicators. Guidance on the application of the *Framework* is provided in the *OFSTED Handbook* (the *Handbook*) which is issued in different versions to cater for the inspection of different types of school.

INSPECTION OUTCOMES

5 Inspection must lead to a full report, together with a summary of the report, which:

i   evaluates the school according to the *Framework*, any amendments required by HMCI, and the contract specification for the individual inspection;

---

[1]   Under the Education Act 1993 (the 1993 Act), pupil referral units (PRUs) are designated as schools. All references to schools include PRUs unless otherwise indicated.

[2]   The 1992 and 1993 Acts, and any subsequent legislation.

ii   identifies the strengths and weaknesses of the school; and

iii   gives the appropriate authority[3] for the school a clear agenda for the action required to improve it.

Inspection reports must follow the order prescribed in the *Framework*.

6   The *Framework* describes the obligations of registered inspectors in terms of both the **principles** portrayed in this section, and the **inspection schedule.** The latter sets out:

i   specific requirements for evaluating and reporting on the work of the school and the standards achieved by its pupils; and

ii   the criteria which form the basis for arriving at judgements. These are listed in the schedule under the heading: "Judgements should be based on the extent to which:"

CODE OF CONDUCT FOR INSPECTORS

7   The right of entry to schools by inspectors brings with it important responsibilities. The code set out below outlines the principles which govern the conduct of inspections. Inspectors should uphold the highest professional standards in relation to all who are involved in the process before, during and after the inspection.

Inspectors should:

- carry out their work with professionalism, integrity and courtesy;

- evaluate the work of the school objectively;

- report honestly and fairly;

- communicate clearly and frankly;

- act in the best interests of the pupils at the school; and

- respect the confidentiality of personal information received during the inspection.

8   When inspecting schools, all registered inspectors must ensure that they and the members of their teams abide by this code of conduct.

---

3   The appropriate authority for a maintained school without a delegated budget is the Local Education Authority (LEA), and for an independent school the proprietor. In all other cases it is the governing body. References to the governing body in this Framework are to be taken in the case of independent schools as references to the proprietor or trustees. For all PRUs the LEA is the appropriate authority.

THE STANDARD AND QUALITY OF INSPECTIONS

9 Registered inspectors must ensure that their judgements are:

i **secure,** in that they are rooted in a substantial evidence base and informed by specified quantitative indicators;

ii **first-hand,** in that they are based largely on direct observation of pupils' and teachers' work;

iii **reliable,** in that they are based on consistent application of the evaluation criteria in the inspection schedule contained in this *Framework*;

iv **valid,** in that they accurately reflect what is actually achieved and provided by the school;

v **comprehensive,** in that they cover all aspects of the school set out in the inspection schedule and in the inspection contract specification; and

vi **corporate,** in that conclusions about the school as a whole reflect the collective view of the inspection team.

THE INSPECTION PROCESS AND SCHOOL IMPROVEMENT

10 The inspection process should help the school to raise educational standards. The governors and staff need to be involved as far as possible in the inspection. Where possible, inspectors should discuss with staff the context of work observed, its purpose, and the reasons why work is undertaken in a particular way. It is good practice for inspectors to test hypotheses with staff before judgements are finalised. In that an inspection, of necessity, takes place over a short period of time, inspectors should consider the school's own priorities for development, evidence about the past attainments of pupils and any evidence from the school's own analysis of its provision and standards.

EQUAL OPPORTUNITIES

11 Throughout the inspection, the requirements of the schedule should be applied in relation to **all** pupils in the school. Inspectors must ensure that the full range of age, gender, attainment, special educational need, ethnicity and background is taken into account, including the provision for, and attainment of, pupils having English as an additional language.

TEAM COMPOSITION AND ASSIGNMENTS

12 An inspection must be carried out by a registered inspector assisted by a team of trained inspectors which is sufficient and competent to conduct the inspection according to the requirements of the inspection schedule, unless modified by the contract specification, and Schedule 2 to the 1992 Act. The team must normally be capable of inspecting:

● those aspects of the school specified in the inspection schedule;

- as appropriate: National Curriculum subjects; the curriculum for pupils under five and students post-sixteen; vocational courses; and religious education in those schools which are required by statute to teach the subject according to an Agreed Syllabus[4]; and

- any other subject specified in the inspection contract.

The team must also include one or more inspectors charged with inspecting or co-ordinating the inspection of: equal opportunities issues; and, where relevant, special educational needs, and the education of pupils for whom English is an additional language.

13 In the inspection of primary and special schools, and pupil referral units (PRUs), where teams are small, there must be a combination of phase and subject expertise but without undue fragmentation of the team. **Primary school inspection teams must be competent to inspect the full age range present in the school, including nursery provision.** Teams inspecting special schools or units must include expertise in the main types of special educational need represented as well as the ability to ensure reasonable sampling of the subjects across the age range of pupils at the school.

14 The registered inspector must include in the inspection team at least one member without personal experience in the management of any school or the provision of education in any school: the lay inspector[5]. No aspect of the inspection is to be barred to any inspector.

QUALITY ASSURANCE REQUIREMENTS

15 To ensure that inspections are conducted to the highest standard, contractors for inspections are required to submit to OFSTED details of their quality assurance arrangements. These must cover:

- the induction, support, selection and deployment of inspectors;

- liaison with schools;

- the review and analysis of inspection evidence;

- ensuring that judgements about the school are corporate;

- ensuring the consistency, clarity and accuracy of reports and their compliance with requirements; and

- the use of feedback from the monitoring of inspections by OFSTED.

TIME ALLOCATIONS FOR INSPECTIONS

16 In order to cover the work of the school adequately, **a specified minimum number of inspection days,** including those of the lay inspector, will be spent on direct inspection. The minimum tariff of days on site is set out in the relevant Instruction to Tenderers.

---

4   The 1992 Act as amended by Section 259 of the 1993 Act makes separate provision for the inspection of denominational religious education in those schools where it is provided; such inspections fall under Section 13 of the 1992 Act.

5   Paragraph 3(2) of Schedule 2 to the 1992 Act.

17   Where the inspection contract specifies that there are extra features of the school to be inspected, inspection time beyond the minimum may also be specified. In all inspections, additional time is needed for:

- administration, and preparing for the inspection;

- analysis of documents;

- visiting the school and meeting the staff and governors;

- the pre-inspection meeting with parents;

- collating the findings of team members during and after the inspection;

- discussing findings with those responsible for the school; and

- writing the report and its summary.

THE EVIDENCE BASE

18   The registered inspector must compile, for each inspection, a *Record of Evidence* which contains the evidence collected by each member of the team. The detailed content of the *Record of Evidence* is prescribed in the *Handbook* and *Inspection Resource Pack*. The basic quantitative data about the school summarised in the *Headteacher's Form* are important evidence. The registered inspector is responsible for checking and where necessary correcting the data in the Form. OFSTED also provides data to enable inspectors to set the school's data in a national context.

BEFORE THE INSPECTION

19   The registered inspector must provide the appropriate authority and the headteacher[6] of the school with a list of the information and documents which are needed before the inspection, giving sufficient notice for the school to gather the items together and to complete the *Headteacher's Form* and *Statement*. The documents required are specified in Part II of the *Handbook*. In addition, the registered inspector will need to visit the school and prepare for inspection. The registered inspector should invite the appropriate authority to distribute the parents' questionnaire for return to the inspector before the meeting with parents.

20   The appropriate authority for the school must arrange a meeting between the registered inspector and those parents of pupils at the school who wish to attend[7]. The registered inspector should ensure that parents' views are sought on aspects of the school specified in the *Handbook*. Parents' views contribute to the inspection evidence and must be taken into account in the course of the inspection. As the meeting takes place before the inspection, the registered inspector will not be able to comment on parents' views of the school. The registered inspector should discuss with the

---

6   Or teacher in charge.

7   Schedule 2 to the 1992 Act.

headteacher and the appropriate authority the key matters raised through the questionnaire and at the meeting. Where inspection reports refer to views expressed by parents, they should indicate the extent to which inspection findings support those views.

DURING THE INSPECTION

21 The sample of work inspected in a school must constitute an adequate cross-section. Wherever possible, the classes and work seen, and interviews with pupils, must be representative of all ages and levels of attainment. Work should be inspected in National Curriculum subjects as appropriate and in any other subjects or aspects specified in the inspection contract. Where a subject is not being taught at the time of the inspection, the report should state this fact clearly. In such a case, evaluation of pupils' attainment and progress in the subject should be based on the work previously completed by pupils, if this constitutes a sufficient sample, together with such other evidence as may be available. Members of the team should inspect the whole range of the school's work including extra-curricular activities. The inspection team should inspect acts of worship, except in schools where collective worship falls to be inspected under Section 13 of the 1992 Act[8] or where collective worship is not required.

22 The overall findings of the inspection should reflect the balance of evidence provided by the inspection team. The **Main Findings** and the **Key Issues for Action** must represent a corporate view.

23 Towards the end of the inspection it will be necessary for the registered inspector to ensure that all team members have indicated their evaluations clearly, and, with the team, to consider whether or not the school is failing, or likely to fail, to give its pupils an acceptable standard of education and thus requires special measures. The procedures to be adopted in such cases and the criteria on which to base a conclusion that a school falls into this category are set out in Annex 1 to this *Framework* and amplified in Part II of the *Handbook*.

AFTER THE INSPECTION

24 The registered inspector must offer to discuss the findings of the inspection first with the headteacher, who may invite any staff of the school to be present. The appropriate authority must also be offered an oral report. This should occur as soon as possible after the inspection and before the inspection report is finalised. The registered inspector should present the findings of the report in such a way that they can easily be assimilated, for example, by using visual aids. The purpose of these discussions is not only to share with those concerned the outcomes of the inspection but to provide an opportunity for clarification of the Main Findings and Key Issues for Action.

25 It is also important to check on the factual accuracy of the inspection report. This is best done by offering the pre-publication text of the written report to the school after oral reports have been completed. Factual errors must be corrected. Only if such errors have a direct bearing on particular inspection judgements should the inspection team consider revising their judgements. Otherwise, there must be no modification of the judgements in the report.

---

8   See footnote 4 on page 11

THE INSPECTION REPORT AND SUMMARY

26   The written report and a summary must be prepared by the registered inspector and sent to the appropriate authority for the school before the end of the period specified by HMCI in the inspection contract. Copies should also be sent to those specified in Section 209 of the 1993 Act or paragraph 9c of Schedule 2 to the 1992 Act. The report must be written in the order of the inspection schedule.

27   The summary of the report should reproduce the Main Findings and Key Issues for Action sections of the inspection report together with a very brief contextual statement about the school indicating its type and size, a summary of the response to the parents' questionnaire, and the standard text specified in the *Handbook*.

28   The inspection report and summary and those parts of the *Record of Evidence* required by HMCI must also be sent to OFSTED. Inspectors should retain their complete *Record of Evidence* for 12 months from the date of inspection. OFSTED may call on this record at any time during that period.

MONITORING

29   When an inspection is to be monitored by OFSTED to assess compliance of the registered inspector with the specified inspection procedures, the registered inspector will be notified and must afford HMI all necessary co-operation. HMI have access to all elements of the inspection.

Note: The Inspection Schedule is integrated in Part III of this Handbook: 'The Inspection Schedule and Guidance on its use'.

ANNEX 1

SCHOOLS REQUIRING SPECIAL MEASURES

1 Consideration of whether a school is failing, or likely to fail, to give its pupils an acceptable standard of education and therefore requires special measures should be based on the extent to which some or all of the following characteristics relating to the different sections of the Schedule are evident in the school.

Educational standards achieved

◆ low attainment and poor progress in the subjects of the curriculum by the majority of pupils or consistently among particular groups of pupils. This will be evident in poor examination, National Curriculum assessment and other accredited results;

◆ regular disruptive behaviour, breakdown of discipline or high levels of exclusions;

◆ significant levels of racial tension or harassment; and

◆ poor attendance by a substantial proportion of pupils or by particular groups of pupils, or high levels of truancy.

Quality of education provided

◆ a high proportion of unsatisfactory teaching, including low expectations of pupils;

◆ failure to implement the National Curriculum;

◆ very poor provision for pupils' spiritual, moral, social and cultural development;

◆ pupils at physical or emotional risk from other pupils or adults in the school; and

◆ abrasive and confrontational relationships between staff and pupils.

The management and efficiency of the school

◆ ineffectiveness of the headteacher, senior management or governors;

◆ significant loss of confidence in the headteacher by the staff, parents or governors;

◆ demoralisation and disenchantment amongst staff or high levels of staff turnover or absence;

◆ poor management and inefficient use made of the resources, including finance, available to the school; and

◆ poor value for money provided by the school.

2   A decision that a school requires special measures will depend on the combined weight of features. It is unlikely that one feature alone will result in such a decision, but where there is widespread and significantly poor attainment and progress, risk to pupils or the likelihood of a breakdown of discipline, the school will normally be judged to require special measures. In all such cases the headteacher and the governing body should be informed of the registered inspector's concern.

3   Where a judgement is made that the school is failing or likely to fail to give its pupils an acceptable standard of education, the registered inspector has a duty to inform HMCI and express the opinion in the report stating whether or not HMCI agrees. Further guidance on the procedures to be followed are included in Part II of the *Handbook*.

PART II

GUIDANCE ON INSPECTION REQUIREMENTS: THE CONDUCT OF INSPECTIONS

This part of the *Handbook* provides guidance on the management and conduct of inspections in line with the inspection requirements set out in the Framework. It is structured to reflect the sequence of work before, during and after the time the inspection team spends in the school.

Responsibility for the conduct and management of the inspection, and for the inspection report, rests with the registered inspector named in the contract. While this guidance focuses on the role of the registered inspector, it is important that all team members are aware of the inspection requirements and comply with them, particularly the Code of Conduct.

CODE OF CONDUCT FOR INSPECTORS

1   The *Framework* includes a Code of Conduct which is a set of principles and must govern the conduct of inspections. The principles should be followed by all inspectors throughout the inspection process, and underpin the high standards of conduct which are expected of those involved in the inspection of a school. Breach of the code is a serious matter, and could in extreme cases result in the loss of registration. Amplification of the Code of Conduct follows.

Inspectors should carry out their work with professionalism, integrity and courtesy.

2   All inspectors need to recognise that the process of inspection is demanding for schools, and that it can be very stressful. The way in which the inspection is conducted should contribute to reducing any stress to a minimum. The conduct of inspectors should instil confidence, minimise disruption and anxiety and ensure the co-operation of staff and members of the appropriate authority. Inspectors should be well-briefed and treat all those involved with the school with respect.

3   Inspectors must carry out their statutory duties and maintain their independence and objectivity, and that of OFSTED. The term 'registered inspector' must be used only in connection with inspections undertaken for OFSTED. Inspectors must not use their position as inspectors to secure further employment where it may reflect on their impartiality or compromise the integrity of the inspection. In contributing to educational debate or working in other professional capacities, inspectors must not undermine their capacity to conduct inspections for OFSTED.

Inspectors should evaluate the work of the school objectively.

4   The inspection has to be undertaken without bias or preconceptions about the school. No inspector should take part in an inspection if they have a close previous relationship with the school. Inspectors must be absolutely impartial, and be seen to be impartial, in their treatment of all those with whom they come into contact. Judgements must be based on sound evidence which has been carefully weighed, collected from a range of sources and firmly based on the criteria in the inspection schedule. Inspectors must be particularly careful to avoid making premature judgements.

Inspectors should report honestly and fairly.

5   Inspectors must report on their findings without fear or favour. They must report on positive features and strengths, but must not refrain from identifying and reporting on difficult issues which will need resolution for the school to improve. When inspectors come to their conclusions, issues need to be considered carefully and minor issues should not be given undue prominence. The resulting report should be as fair and just a representation of the school as possible, with all recommendations firmly supported by evidence. The oral reports of inspection findings to staff and members of the appropriate authority must be consistent with the final report.

Inspectors should communicate clearly and frankly.

6   Inspectors must maintain an open dialogue with all those involved in the school without compromising the confidentiality of information about individuals. Parents, teachers and other staff, pupils and members of the appropriate authority need to understand fully the purposes of inspection, the role they play in the process and what is required of them.

7   Good communication is particularly important during the oral reports to staff and the appropriate authority. Complex information and possibly unwelcome judgements should be conveyed as simply and accessibly as possible.

Inspectors should act in the best interests of the pupils at the school.

8   Inspectors enter schools in a position of authority, and the safety and well-being of the pupils must be a prime concern. Nothing an inspector does should cause a child distress or anxiety. Inspectors should ensure that no situation arises which could be construed as calling into question the propriety of the relationship between inspector and pupil, for example, talking to individual pupils in isolation or singling out individual pupils for undue attention.

9   If inspectors observe or hear of anything which causes them concern about the safety or well-being of the pupils then the registered inspector must report these concerns to the headteacher or appropriate authority. If, in the interests of the safety and well-being of the pupils, the registered inspector deems it inappropriate to do so, then he or she must inform the appropriate external agency, for example, where relevant, the Social Services Department. If indiscipline or bad behaviour of pupils is observed when a teacher is present, an inspector should not interfere unless the safety or welfare of pupils is endangered.

Inspectors should respect the confidentiality of personal information received during the inspection.

10   Inspectors will be privy to information about individuals during the inspection. Such information is confidential. The identification of individuals for criticism should not form any part of the formal inspection report or of the discussion with the appropriate authority and this confidentiality must be respected after the inspection. During the course of their work inspectors should not seek access to confidential staff appraisal information; this is not part of the inspection.

11   The findings of the inspection are confidential to the team and the school until the final report is published.

THE EVIDENCE BASE

12   Systematic collection and evaluation of evidence is at the heart of inspection. A key part of the registered inspector's role is to manage the evidence base and ensure that sound and fair judgements derive from it. The nature of the *Record of Evidence* of inspection which registered inspectors will assemble before and during the inspection is outlined below. Further guidance on this is included in the *Inspection Resource Pack* for inspectors.

THE RECORD OF EVIDENCE

13   The registered inspectors must compile for each inspection a *Record of Evidence* (*RoE*) which summarises all the relevant evidence collected by the inspection team. The *RoE* should:

i   provide a format for recording the key inspection evidence in a form which assists writing the report;

ii   secure the evidence on which judgements in the report are based in case of legal challenge;

iii   enable HMCI to have access to a formal *RoE* as part of OFSTED's quality assurance procedures.

14   OFSTED will retrieve from inspection reports and use parts of the *RoE* to provide a national evidence base to inform HMCI's Annual Report[9] and other reports on aspects of the education system.

15   The *Record of Evidence* consists of:

Data from OFSTED

This may include a Pre-inspection Context and School Indicator (PICSI) report containing key performance data about the school from earlier years to enable trends to be identified; information about the social and economic characteristics of the area in which the school is situated; and comparative data to help inspectors set the school data in a national context.

The Headteacher's Form and Statement[10]

A minimum core of quantitative data about the school, provided in standard format, together with the headteacher's commentary on the school which should include a brief description of the characteristics of the school, its pupils, and those features of the area it serves which influence its work.

---

[9]   As required by the 1992 Act.

[10]   References to headteacher include the teacher in charge of a pupil referral unit (PRU).

The Observation Form

A basis for recording evidence and judgements from the observation of lessons and other inspection activities, including scrutiny of pupils' work, discussion with pupils and analysis of assessment and examination data.

The Subject Profile

A summary which draws together the evidence for each subject inspected, and a set of grades to reflect judgements in each subject.

The School Profile

A summary which draws together the evidence compiled by the team of inspectors during the inspection; and a set of grades to reflect the corporate judgements of the inspection team.

Any Other Evidence

Any other working notes that the registered inspector wishes to retain within the *RoE*.

BEFORE THE INSPECTION

INITIAL CONTACT WITH THE SCHOOL

16   First contacts, written and spoken, between the registered inspector and the school are particularly important in establishing a good working relationship and setting the tone and style for the whole inspection process. They also provide a first insight into the nature of the school.

17   The registered inspector should make contact with the appropriate authority[11], usually via the headteacher, to agree dates for the beginning and end of the inspection. These should be confirmed in writing. Any difficulties should be resolved by negotiation, but in the unlikely event that agreement cannot be reached, OFSTED should be informed. OFSTED will then seek views and fix the date.

18   The registered inspector should subsequently contact the headteacher to:

i   arrange an initial visit to the school, discuss its purpose, and negotiate a programme;

ii   offer to meet the teaching and non-teaching staff during the initial visit to discuss the inspection process and explain the coverage of the curriculum and other aspects of the school's work;

iii offer a meeting to discuss the inspection process with representatives of the appropriate authority. Normally this will occur during the initial visit; and

iv   discuss the information which will be required from the school before the inspection, explaining why it is needed, and make arrangements for its collection.

---

[11]   The appropriate authority is usually the governing body of the school, but in schools without a fully delegated budget and in PRUs it is the LEA.

The following should be requested, as appropriate:

- a completed *Headteacher's Form* and *Statement*;

- school prospectus;

- school development plan or equivalent planning document;

- copy of last annual report to parents (not required for PRUs);

- minutes of meetings of the appropriate authority for the last 12 months (copy of any reports to LEA by teacher in charge of a PRU);

- staff handbook (if available);

- curriculum policies, plans and schemes of work, already in existence ;

- other policy documents which are available in the school;

- a timetable of the work of the school for the period of the inspection; and

- other information the school wishes to be considered, including any documents about, and the outcomes of, any school self-evaluation activities.

If the inspection is to take place early in the school year, the registered inspector should advise the school that pupils' work from the previous year will be needed.

19 The registered inspector should send the *Headteacher's Form* and *Statement* to the school for completion before the initial visit. Where a PICSI report is provided by OFSTED, this should also be sent to the school for discussion during the initial visit.

20 It is important that schools do not feel that substantial documentation must be produced specially for the inspection. Some additional items, for example, attendance registers, samples of pupils' records and reports to parents, may be required by inspectors during the week of the inspection, often to be used in conjunction with the samples of pupils' work. **On no account should inspectors issue additional forms to the school for completion, beyond those prescribed by OFSTED.**

21 The registered inspector should remind the headteacher that the appropriate authority must inform interested parties in the local community of the inspection and invite their views on the school. Outside bodies include the local Training and Enterprise Council (TEC) and representatives of the local business community, including significant employers who have recently employed former pupils of the school. Any views on the school should be sent to the registered inspector.

INITIAL VISIT

22 The initial visit to the school should be carefully planned through discussion with the head and arranged at a mutually convenient time.

23   The registered inspector should explain to the school that analysis of the school's documentation and other information collected during the initial visit is used to give other members of the team a background to the inspection and to help the registered inspector to identify any particular issues on which the inspection might focus. The registered inspector should invite the headteacher and appropriate authority to identify particular aspects that they would like inspectors to focus on, provided this can be done within the scope of the *Framework* and the contract.

24   During the initial visit, the registered inspector should:

i   discuss with the headteacher the inspection process, including lesson observation procedures and other aspects of methodology, and post-inspection events;

ii   confirm the composition of the inspection team, provide information about how the team will be deployed and discuss coverage of the curriculum and other aspects of the school's work. The contract provides for the registered inspector to supply the school with a brief summary of the background of the team members. If for any reason it is not possible to detail the team deployment at the time of the initial visit this should be done as soon as possible after the visit. In any case it must be done in accordance with the timtetable set out in the contract;

iii   resolve any difficulties the headteacher may have found in completing the *Headteacher's Form* and *Statement*;

iv   if a PICSI report has been provided, check it with the headteacher for any inconsistencies and begin to form a description of the characteristics of the school (section 3.1 of the report) for agreement with the headteacher and appropriate authority;

v   collect the documentation requested;

vi   agree the additional information to be made available during the inspection, for example:

◆ samples of pupils' work;

◆ pupils' records and reports;

◆ any individual education plans;

◆ teachers' planning and assessment documents, including schemes of work if not provided earlier;

◆ registers of attendance; and

◆ any other information the school feels would be helpful to the inspection;

vii   gather pre-inspection evidence for the *School Profile* through discussion with the headteacher, other staff and representatives of the appropriate authority if available;

viii   arrange for the whole school or subject/class timetables to be provided, if not made available earlier. Any likely changes to the timetable or significant disruption of it should be discussed. Inspectors should expect to see teaching in the National Curriculum subjects and other subjects or courses that are part of its normal programme as specified in the contract;

ix   give a clear indication of the kind of discussions likely to be required with individual members of staff, keeping demands on their time to a minimum, especially where they carry multiple responsibilities. Where it is possible to agree a programme of discussions with key staff in advance of inspection, this should be done;

x   discuss arrangements for looking at pupils' samples of work, including any particular arrangements needed where, for example, the inspection is at the start of a new year;

xi   in the case of a PRU, arrange visits to schools where pupils have dual registration to discuss liaison arrangements. Such visits should only be undertaken with the agreement of the appropriate authority of the school to be visited;

xii   meet the staff to explain how the inspection will be conducted and how feedback will be given to teachers.

25   At or before the initial visit, the registered inspector needs to negotiate with the headteacher the date and time for the pre-inspection meeting with parents to seek their views of the school. It is important to note that:

◆   the appropriate authority is responsible for arranging the meeting;

◆   the meeting should be held before the inspection;

◆   parents should be given three weeks' notice of the meeting;

◆   all parents of pupils registered at the school at the time of the inspection should be invited.

A sample letter, including a suggested agenda for the meeting, to be used by the appropriate authority for inviting parents to the meeting, is included in the *Inspection Resource Pack*.

26   A standard questionnaire for parents is included in the *Inspection Resource Pack* and inspectors should encourage schools to use this. If the school agrees to issue the questionnaire, arrangements should be made for its return, in confidence, to the registered inspector. The questionnaire should be issued to the parents of all pupils on the roll of the school. The registered inspector should make it clear that a summary of parents' responses will be included in the inspection report.

27   The consensus of views expressed by parents in the meeting and through the questionnaires should be shared with the school and the appropriate authority.

28   The registered inspector should also, at the initial visit, discuss with the headteacher the practicalities of giving oral reports of the inspection findings. Oral reports must be offered to the headteacher, who may invite other staff to be present, and subsequently to the appropriate authority. Mutually convenient dates will need to be arranged for these meetings. Inspectors should discuss with the headteacher the appropriateness and practicality of sharing findings with staff holding positions of responsibility.

29   During the initial visit it is particularly useful for the registered inspector to be shown around the school to meet staff and pupils, become familiar with the site(s) and gain first impressions of the school to provide the team with a background to their visit.

30   The registered inspector should discuss courtesies and domestic arrangements, for example the introduction of team members to the school, access to the building outside normal school hours and a base for the team. Schools will normally provide a meeting room for inspectors, if this is not possible the registered inspector should arrange to use suitable accommodation nearby.

PREPARING THE TEAM FOR INSPECTION

31   The registered inspector is responsible for ensuring that members of the team are thoroughly prepared for the inspection and that their work is well planned. It is important that teams establish a corporate approach and style which are maintained with consistency.

Deployment of the team

32   Within the scope of the contract, the registered inspector should plan and agree with the team members a realistic allocation of responsibilities to ensure that:

i   the full range of subjects, vocational courses and aspects specified in the schedule and the contract are covered by inspectors with suitable expertise. In order to achieve specialist coverage, the inspection team will include a number of full-time members inspecting and co-ordinating aspects in addition to their own subjects, possibly with some specialist inspectors who will spend less time in the school;

ii   sufficient time is available to inspectors which will allow adequate sampling of work. In a vocational subject this may include off-site learning, although inspection should not be undertaken in another school unless this is part of the inspection contract. The time available for subject inspection will vary according to the size of the department. For inspectors in the school for a short time, particular care must be taken in planning to ensure that a representative coverage of lessons will be possible;

iii the lay inspector is given assignments across a range of aspects of the school's work to allow a full contribution to be made to the inspection and the corporate judgements; and

iv   the team is informed of any pre-inspection and post-inspection team meetings and deadlines for writing.

Pre-inspection analysis

33   The pre-inspection sections of the *School Profile* must be completed to provide a brief commentary for the team and to identify inspection issues specific to the school. This should take account of any significant points from the initial visit or raised at the parents' meeting, the outcome of any self-evaluation measures, issues for inspection identified by the school, and analyses of the PICSI report and other information. Any views expressed by the TEC and representatives of the local community, including employers, should be considered in the same way as parents' views. The *School Profile* should place a PRU within the context of LEA policy and should include the number of pupils re-integrated into schools in the last academic year.

Briefing the team

34   Through a meeting, or by other means, the registered inspector should:

i   ensure that the team is thoroughly briefed about the school and the inspection, and receives all pre-inspection comments and analyses;

ii   distribute copies of documentation relating to areas of responsibility of team members;

iii   draw up a programme for the inspection, including any inspection activities in which several team members may need to take part. The registered inspector may wish to ask team members to draw up individual plans for the inspection of subjects or aspects. Care should be taken to ensure representative coverage of year groups, key stages, ability groupings and other activities connected, for example, with vocational courses;

iv   ensure that team members understand the arrangements made for the scrutiny of pupils' work;

v   prepare timetables and agendas for team meetings, including the arrangements for securing corporate judgements;

vi   arrange for at least one member of the team to accompany the registered inspector to meetings with the headteacher and appropriate authority for oral reporting; and

vii   establish clear procedures for ensuring adherence to the Code of Conduct for inspectors.

THE PARENTS' MEETING

35   The parents' meeting is an opportunity to inform parents about the inspection and to fulfil the statutory requirement to seek parents' views on the school. The registered inspector should be accompanied by a member of the inspection team to record the views of parents. The meeting can only be attended by parents of pupils registered at the school at the time of the inspection. Members of the staff and the appropriate authority may attend only if they have a child currently attending the school. The headteacher or chair of the appropriate authority may, of course, wish to be present at the start of the meeting to introduce the registered inspector.

36   The registered inspector should:

i   explain the purpose of the meeting and provide an agenda;

ii   explain and answer questions on the nature of the inspection and the report;

iii   seek parents' views about the school and its context; and

iv   note, but make no comment on the validity of those views.

37   The registered inspector should make clear at the start of the meeting that parents' views will be taken into account as part of the inspection. Parents should be asked to couch their comments in general terms as far as possible, and avoid naming individuals.

38   The registered inspector should seek parents' views on:

i   pupils' attainment and progress;

ii   the attitudes and values which the school promotes;

iii   the information which the school provides for parents, including reports;

iv   the help and guidance available to pupils;

v   homework and the contribution it makes to pupils' progress;

vi   pupils' behaviour and attendance;

vii   the part parents play in the life of the school; and

viii   the school's response to their suggestions and complaints.

DURING THE INSPECTION

THE ROLE OF THE REGISTERED INSPECTOR

39   The registered inspector is the manager of the inspection team and the whole inspection process, and is the first point of reference for everyone involved in the inspection. Effective management and organisation of the team on a day-to-day basis are crucial to the success of the inspection. It is the registered inspector's responsibility to ensure that judgements are secure, first-hand, reliable, valid, comprehensive and corporate. The registered inspector is also responsible for producing the inspection report and the summary of the report. These must be clear and helpful to the appropriate authority and parents.

40   The registered inspector should:

i   ensure that inspectors are consistent in their approaches to the collection and recording of evidence;

ii   be prepared to adjust the workload of individual inspectors as circumstances dictate;

iii   monitor and, if necessary, intervene in the work of the team so as to ensure compliance with the *Framework*;

iv   undertake direct inspection such as observing work in classrooms, sampling pupils' written work, and holding discussions with staff and pupils; and

v   provide systems for the collection, collation and validation of evidence within the team; review and analyse this evidence, keeping the *Record of Evidence* up to date.

41   The registered inspector should meet the headteacher regularly to agree administrative details, obtain further information, clarify inspection issues and resolve difficulties which might emerge during the inspection.

TEAM INSPECTORS' ASSIGNMENTS

42   Inspectors need to plan and use their time carefully and efficiently to achieve the coverage required, but they should be sensitive to the impact of the inspection on teaching and staff. Inspection of some aspects of the school's work will require contributions from the whole team, and will need to be co-ordinated by one of the inspectors. Such aspects include, for example, the assessment of:

i   the quality of provision for, and standards achieved by, pupils with special educational needs;

ii   equality of opportunity for different groups of pupils;

iii pupils' spiritual, moral, social and cultural development.

43   Inspectors need to draw evidence relating to their subject from across the curriculum. So, for example, the inspector co-ordinating the inspection of English will need to take account of pupils' competence in reading, writing, speaking and listening and opportunities for them in subjects other than English. This will require contributions from other inspectors. Similarly the inspectors co-ordinating the inspection of mathematics and information technology will need to take account of numeracy and information technology capability across the curriculum when assessing attainment and progress and quality of provision in those subjects.

GATHERING THE INSPECTION EVIDENCE

44   Within their assignments individual inspectors should allocate time to collect the range of core evidence on which the judgements of the team must be based. This includes:

i   the inspection of teaching and of pupils at work in classrooms and other areas, including work off-site where the inspection priorities allow, where there is agreement with the appropriate authority and where it is practicable and manageable;

ii   discussion with pupils, for example, to assess their understanding and knowledge of different subjects and their attitudes to work and their life at school;

iii the scrutiny of samples of pupils' work within individual subject areas as well as contributing to the scrutiny of all the work of selected pupils in their work across the curriculum;

iv   discussion with staff, especially those with management responsibilities, such as heads of department;

v   the scrutiny of schemes of work and teachers' plans, records of National Curriculum tests and teachers' assessments, and results in GCSE, A-level, GNVQ and other courses, and details of any assessment undertaken on entry, and other measures or indicators of attainment and progress used by the school;

vi   the scrutiny of statements of special educational need, individual education plans, annual reviews; and

vii with the agreement of the appropriate authority and where possible, visiting a small sample of schools where dual registration or re-integration of pupils attending a PRU is taking place.

The evidence should be recorded on *Observation Forms* as the inspection proceeds. A complete specification of evidence is given earlier in this part of the *Handbook* (Paragraphs 12-15).

Review of documentary evidence

45   Documentary evidence provided by the school must be assimilated and fully considered. Analysis of material prior to inspection forms the basis of pre-inspection commentaries relating to aspects

of the *Framework*. Other documentary evidence is needed during the inspection, for example, pupils' records and reports. Time should be set aside during the inspection for consideration of this material.

46   Statements of aims, policies and documents relating to procedures should be evaluated in terms of their impact on the work of the school. Inspectors should determine whether intentions are followed through into effective practice.

Careful analysis should be undertaken of assessment and examination results to provide evidence of attainment and trends in performance over time.

Observation of lessons and other activities

47   While the school is in session the inspection team should aim to spend at least 60% of its time observing lessons, sampling pupils' work and talking to pupils.

48   Observation of lessons should include sufficient work in each key stage and post-16 and adequate time should be spent in lessons to provide the basis for valid and reliable judgements to be made. Inevitably, there will be variation in the time spent in lessons, but some whole lessons should be observed. Lessons or sessions observed should be from the normal programme of work; inspectors should not impose or require changes to that programme.

49   Effective inspection involves joining individual pupils and groups to look at their work and to discuss it with them. It also includes careful observation of teaching, including the organisation of work for pupils as a class, in groups or individually. Both need to be done so as not to disrupt either teaching or learning, and note-taking should be as unobtrusive as possible.

50   Where possible all teachers should be visited when teaching, whatever the size of the school. The load on teachers should be spread as evenly as possible. Inspectors should visit classes taught by supply teachers or students in training; in these cases the criteria applied for evaluation are the same as for classes taught by established teachers.

51   There should not normally be more than one inspector in a class at any time unless the class teacher agrees and there is a particular reason for so doing, such as tracking the progress of a pupil with special educational needs.

52   Inspection should include assemblies, extra curricular activities, including sport, if offered, and form or tutorial periods. It may also include field work, educational visits and work experience where justifiable and practicable.

Talking with pupils

53   Evidence of pupils' attainment and their attitudes to learning derives from discussions with them. Talking to pupils is helpful in judging the extent of their understanding of current and recent work, and their ability to apply knowledge in different contexts. This discussion will often happen as inspectors join individual pupils or groups of pupils at work. Some structured discussions will also take place with pupils outside lessons.

54   In all classroom observations, it is important to listen to:

- pupils' incidental talk and comments;

- their contribution in class;

- their responses to questions;

- the questions initiated by them; and

- their views, feelings and comments expressed in discussions.

Sampling pupils' work

55   Pupils' previous and current work provide an essential source of evidence of both attainment and progress, as well as an insight into the curriculum and teaching. In addition to the work routinely seen during the observation of lessons, inspectors will need to look at the samples of work agreed between the registered inspector and the headteacher during the initial visit.

56   It is helpful if the sampling takes place near the beginning of the week in order to follow up the issues raised. Judgements on the sample should be made in relation to other work observed during the inspection.

57   The sample should include:

i   the work of at least three pupils in each year group. The sample should include one pupil from each group of pupils of above average, average and below average attainment. The post-16 sample should include the work of a representative number of students following different courses;

ii   the work of any pupils with statements of special educational needs.

58   For each pupil, examples of past and present work should be available in order to establish the range of work covered over time and to evaluate evidence of progress. Inspectors will find it helpful to have pupils' records available alongside their written work, including individual education plans or statements of special educational need. It is also helpful to follow up the scrutiny of this work through discussion with the pupils. In a PRU, it is helpful if salient points in the pupils' educational history, the pupils' individual education plans, the date of admission to the unit, and whether placement is full or part-time, are provided alongside the samples of work.

Discussion with staff, the appropriate authority and others involved in the work of the school

59   Headteachers and registered inspectors alike value a daily meeting to agree administrative details, discuss any matters of concern, clarify inspection issues and obtain further information. These contribute a great deal to the smooth running of an inspection and the maintenance of good relationships.

60   Discussions with the headteacher, representatives of the appropriate authority, staff with particular management responsibilities and class teachers provide important sources of evidence relating to roles and responsibilities, procedures and policies. They are also essential to the professional dialogue between staff and inspectors which contributes positively to the inspection of schools and helps inspectors to establish the context of what is seen. Discussion with teachers, especially at the end of lessons or sessions, is always desirable, but it may not always be possible to have more than a brief exchange. However, the work of teachers should be acknowledged and as many opportunities as possible found for professional dialogue. Such dialogue might involve clarification of the context of the lesson or session, and of future work, as well as providing brief evaluation of the quality of work seen in the lesson, where this is possible. Inspectors should not, however, allow discussion about the work and its evaluation to stray into giving on-the-spot advice, nor adopt an advisory role in any part of the inspection.

61   Meetings with staff and representatives of the appropriate authority about their areas of responsibility should be arranged at mutually convenient times, preferably through negotiation before the start of the inspection. Where possible a list of points to form the focus of the discussion should be indicated in advance, to give those concerned time to think about the issues. Care should be taken that meetings do not make unreasonable demands on teachers' time, for instance their break times. Careful planning and co-ordination of meetings with staff who have several responsibilities are required to ensure efficient use of time.

62   Discussions with non-teaching staff, voluntary helpers and any visiting specialists, eg. speech therapists, are also a valuable source of information and contribute to involving all staff in the inspection.

ORAL REPORTING TO HEADS OF DEPARTMENT AND OTHER TEACHERS WITH SIGNIFICANT RESPONSIBILITIES

63   Towards the end of the inspection, oral reports on the inspection findings in particular subjects or aspects of the schools' work should be offered, where appropriate, to those with significant responsibilities. In most schools it should be possible to provide feedback to subject heads of department, staff with a key responsibility for pupils' welfare and course co-ordinators; and the school may wish other staff, including senior management staff, to be present. It is important that the format and arrangements for oral reporting are consistent across the school and fully understood. Where possible, they should be negotiated with the school before the inspection. A clear understanding should be reached as to who receives feedback. Specific issues relating to a particular lesson or observed practice which could be identified with a teacher must not be raised with the head of department unless the issue has also been raised with the particular teacher concerned. Similarly, those with responsibility for, for example, subject areas, should be aware of issues in the subject which will be raised with the headteacher.

64   The registered inspector should ensure that the school understands that issues may be discussed with those immediately involved in a particular subject, course or aspect of work, and factual issues may be clarified, but judgements are not negotiable.

DATA MANAGEMENT

65 During the inspection the registered inspector will need to manage and analyse the data gathered by the team in order to:

i monitor and ensure appropriate coverage of subjects, courses, year groups, key stages, and different ability groups; and

ii provide a picture of the emerging evidence, to inform team discussion and the making of corporate judgements.

HEALTH AND SAFETY

66 It is unlikely that the registered inspector is an expert in health and safety matters. Inspectors are not therefore required to carry out an audit of health and safety practice. The registered inspector must, however, record and report on those aspects of the school which, in his or her opinion constitute a threat to health and safety.

67 In order to meet these requirements the registered inspector should:

i check that the school is aware of the need to comply with statutory requirements for health and safety[12] and has clear procedures to identify and control health and safety risks;

ii comment on any health and safety risks observed during inspection;

iii record any health and safety irregularities and bring these to the attention of the headteacher and the employer[13]; and

iv alert the Health and Safety Executive where there is an imminent risk of serious injury and the employer appears likely to refuse to remedy the situation.

68 The registered inspector must not only ascertain that the school has a health and safety policy and is aware of statutory requirements but should also judge whether the school has a responsible attitude towards the education and training of pupils in safe practice. Further guidance on Health and Safety matters is included in Part III of the *Handbook*. Additionally, references relating to Health and Safety issues in science, design and technology, physical education and art are included in Part III.

---

[12] Detailed commentary on the statutory requirements for health and safety in schools and on how schools should manage these aspects can be found in the HSE publication *Managing Health and Safety*, ISBN 0-71-760770-4.

[13] The Health and Safety at Work (HSW) Act 1974 places certain responsibilities on employers, which will differ according to the type of school. In county, controlled and special agreement schools the employer is the local education authority (LEA). The governing body is the employer in aided, self-governing grant-maintained schools and city technology colleges. In some independent schools the school proprietor is the employer. Inspectors should refer to the relevant edition of the DFE publication *School Governors: A Guide to the Law*.

TEAM MEETINGS

69   The main purpose of team meetings is to arrive at an accurate and thoroughly tested corporate view of pupils' attainments and progress and the factors which contribute to or detract from these outcomes, i.e. the quality of education provided, provision for pupils' spiritual, moral, social and cultural development, how well the school is led and whether its resources are managed efficiently.

70   Well-structured and managed meetings help a team to give proper consideration to the evidence, to address the judgements required by the *Framework* and to spend time discussing issues which are particularly important.

71   Registered inspectors should establish at these meetings a sense of common purpose, based on good working relationships, and a clear understanding of respective responsibilities within the team.

72   Where the size of team and duration of inspection allow, registered inspectors should establish a programme of team meetings with clear agendas. Opportunities should be provided for:

i   discussion of emerging issues which require the attention of the whole team, such as the standards of oracy or writing across the curriculum, use of support staff, the effects of withdrawing pupils from lessons, or pupils' spiritual, moral, social and cultural development;

ii   the resolution of issues identified earlier as requiring a particular focus during inspection;

iii   an exchange of information as part of each individual inspector's evidence base;

iv   discussion of any weakness or gaps in the evidence base, and how to fill them;

v   consideration of evidence which contributes to main inspection findings and key issues for action;

vi   discussion of evidence and judgements to ensure consistency, and resolution of conflicts where they arise; and

vii   consideration, as a team, of whether the school is failing or likely to fail to give its pupils an acceptable standard of education.

CORPORATE JUDGEMENTS

73   The sharing and testing of hypotheses and inspection issues will inform the corporate work of the team. The registered inspector should ensure that the overall judgements about the school command the agreement of the inspection team. These corporate judgements can most easily be reached through discussion involving all team members towards the end of the inspection. Ultimately the registered inspector must adjudicate, if necessary, and have the final word on judgements to be included in his or her report.

DETERMINING WHETHER A SCHOOL REQUIRES SPECIAL MEASURES[14]

74 The criteria to be used in determining whether a school is failing or likely to fail to give its pupils an acceptable standard of education are listed in Annex 1 to Part 1 and should be applied carefully. The registered inspector and the team should consider whether the standards of achievement and quality of education are so greatly impaired that many pupils are not receiving the education to which they are entitled or if pupils are at a serious physical or emotional risk from adults in the school or from other pupils. A judgement that a school is failing must not be withheld on the grounds that the school's management is likely at some stage in the future to be able to improve the situation.

75 Where the inspection team considers that the accumulating inspection evidence suggests that the school may require special measures, further guidance may be sought at any time directly from OFSTED. Once the registered inspector and team judge that special measures may be required, the registered inspector should inform the headteacher orally, before leaving the school, that in the opinion of the inspection team there are serious deficiencies and that the team is considering whether the school is failing, or likely to fail, to give its pupils an acceptable standard of education.

76 The registered inspector must come to a judgement about whether the school requires special measures before reporting the inspection findings to senior managers and the appropriate authority and must inform OFSTED before telling the school.

77 Where the inspection team considers that any individual pupil is seriously at risk, action should be taken to inform the headteacher and appropriate authority immediately.

AFTER THE INSPECTION

ORAL REPORTING TO THE HEADTEACHER AND THE APPROPRIATE AUTHORITY

78 The registered inspector, accompanied by one or more team members, must offer to discuss the inspection findings with the headteacher and any other staff of the school whom the head wishes to invite, normally the senior management team.

79 The registered inspector must also offer to meet the appropriate authority to discuss the inspection findings. This meeting is called by the appropriate authority, and its composition is determined by them *but must include the headteacher*. Nothing at the meeting of the appropriate authority should come as a surprise to the headteacher. The appropriate authority of county and voluntary schools can, if they wish, invite representatives of the LEA. The meetings with the headteacher and with the governing body must both take place before the written report is finalised.

---

14 The action set out in paragraph 23 of Part 1 of the Framework is that required under Section 206 (7) of the Education Act 1993.

80   During these meetings the registered inspector should emphasise the following:

i   oral feedback remains confidential and the findings of the inspection must not be released to the press until after the report has been received by the appropriate authority; and

ii   the school should point out any factual errors and these will be corrected in the report; judgements are not negotiable.

81   The quality of feedback is an important factor in influencing how the school responds to the inspection findings, particularly in drawing up its action plan, to improve any areas of weakness. Effective oral feedback:

i   is well-structured, clear, succinct, unrushed and allows opportunities for discussion and clarification;

ii   presents a balanced, rounded picture of the work, giving credit to schools where they do things well and pinpointing any weaknesses.

Registered inspectors should also note that:

i   the purposes of the meetings are to present main findings and key issues and to highlight key areas for action, but not to advise on possible action to be taken;

ii   the meetings provide an opportunity, in covering the management and efficiency of the school, to comment on any self-evaluation or quality assurance processes undertaken by the school;

iii   the text of section 3.1 of the schedule, 'Characteristics of the school', should be agreed with the headteacher and the appropriate authority; and

iv   representatives of the appropriate authority will be better able to follow what is being reported if, for the purposes of the meeting only, they are shown copies of the draft **Main Findings** and **Key Issues for Action** and if the presentation draws on visual aids. It is not necessary to read, word by word, the entire draft report.

82   A draft report must be shown to the school to assist with the checking of factual content but not to have judgements negotiated. The draft report should not be shared in advance of the feedback to the head and appropriate authority. Factual errors identified either during meetings or from the draft report should be corrected.

THE REPORT AND SUMMARY OF THE REPORT

83   The report and summary of the report must communicate unequivocal judgements in straightforward language so that:

i   parents, members of the appropriate authority and the local community can have a clear understanding of the school's strengths and weaknesses; and

ii   the school has a useful basis for subsequent action.

84   The report should reflect the individual school as it is. It must follow the structure and precise headings set out in the inspection schedule but its content, wording and style should not be written to any predetermined formula. Key judgements must be absolutely clear, and consistent with the oral report. Reasons for judgements should be given so that readers understand why the inspection team has arrived at these views. While judgements should be based on the criteria set out in the schedule, the report should focus on strengths and weaknesses. It is not necessary to allude to each and every criterion in the schedule, nor to quote the criteria, parrot-fashion.

85   It is essential that the report makes clear the inspection team's judgements about the educational standards achieved by pupils at the school (sections 4.1 to 4.3). Overall judgements should be illustrated by reference to the strengths and weaknesses in the different subjects of the curriculum and particular comment must be made on the core subjects.

86   The report must explain why the educational standards are as they are. Teaching must be a particular focus but all aspects of provision must be judged only in relation to their effects on standards. Where something is unexceptional, no comment is necessary. Particular strengths and weaknesses, though, need amplification to explain why, for example, mathematics teaching is 'outstanding' or leadership is 'weak.'

87   The choice of adjective is left to the discretion of the registered inspector, except that something judged 'sound' or 'satisfactory' must be better than simply strengths balanced by weaknesses. The teaching of a subject, for example, is satisfactory only if the majority of pupils make adequate progress in lessons.

88   The '**Main Findings of Inspection**' and the '**Key Issues for Action**' are particularly important sections of the report. They constitute the summary of the full report but also form the basis of the summary of the report for parents. These sections need particularly careful drafting in order to communicate effectively to a wide readership. They must draw out the key judgements about the school and leave the school without any doubt about the issues which need to be tackled in order to raise the educational standards achieved and why the inspection team has identified particular issues for action. The contents of these sections of the report must be consistent with, and flow from, the body of the full report.

89   The report, and the summary of the report, should therefore:

i   be clear to all of its readers - the appropriate authority, parents, professionals and the wider public;

ii   concentrate on evaluating rather than describing what is seen;

iii   focus on the educational standards achieved and the factors which impact on standards and quality;

iv   use everyday language, not educational jargon, and be grammatically correct;

v   be concrete and specific;

vi   use sub-headings and bullet points, where they help to make the message clear;

vi   use telling examples drawn from the evidence base in order to make generalisations understandable and to illustrate what is meant by 'good' or 'poor';

vii   employ words and phrases that enliven the report and convey the individual character of the school.

90   The report and summary of the report must be consistent with one another. Readers of the summary report will not necessarily read the full report. The summary report must, therefore, be capable of standing alone as a fair and balanced picture of the school, and the steps needed to improve it.

91   The summary report must include the elements specified in the inspection schedule. The brief contextual statement about the school should be limited to its type and size. In addition the summary report must include the following standard text:

■   at the beginning

'The school was inspected in (*month - year*). This is a summary of the inspector's full report, which can be obtained from the school'.

■   at the end

'The governing body is responsible for drawing up an ACTION PLAN within forty working days of receiving the report, showing what the school is going to do about the issues. This action plan will be circulated to all parents at the school.'

'THE INSPECTION'

'(*Name of school*) was inspected as part of a national programme of school inspection. The purpose is to identify strengths and weaknesses in schools that may improve the quality of education offered and raise the standards achieved by their pupils. The inspection of all schools within a four-year cycle is also designed to give parents more information about their children's schools. A copy of this summary is sent to every family with a child at the school.

The inspection of (*name of school*) took place between (*specify dates*). It was undertaken by an independent team of (*number*) inspectors, led by (*name of RgI*). The inspection was commissioned by the Office for Standards in Education, a department of central government.

The team was required to report on the **standards** achieved by pupils, the **quality of education** provided by the school, the **efficiency** with which financial resources were used and the contribution made by the school to its pupils' **spiritual, moral, social and cultural development**'.

---

92   The report and summary report must be produced within 5 (calendar) weeks from the end of the inspection and forwarded without delay to the appropriate authority, HMCI and persons specified in Section 209 of the 1993 Act (or paragraph 9c of Schedule 2 to the 1992 Act).

93   More detailed guidance on writing the report and some examples of report sections will be provided to inspectors.

DOCUMENTS REQUIRED BY OFSTED

94   Registered inspectors must return material to OFSTED as set out in the Contract, as follows:

- the inspection report and summary;

- text and grades in the *School Profile*;

- grades from the *Subject Profile*;

- codes and grades from the *Observation Forms*; and

- the completed *Headteacher's Form*.

All of the above material is required electronically in the format prescribed by OFSTED.

DOCUMENTS TO BE RETAINED BY REGISTERED INSPECTORS

95   Registered inspectors are required to retain the complete *Record of Evidence* for 12 months from the date of publication of the report. As well as copies of the above, they must therefore keep the following material:

- text from *Observation Forms*, which is not routinely required by OFSTED and can be held within the *RoE* in **manuscript** form;

- text from the *Subject Profile*, which is not routinely required by OFSTED and can be held within the *RoE* in **manuscript** form;

- the *Headteacher's Statement* and PICSI Report; and

- any other evidence the registered inspector wishes to retain.

On request, inspectors must send some or all of this material to OFSTED at any time during the 12-month period after the report is published.

SCHOOLS REQUIRING SPECIAL MEASURES

96   Where a school is deemed to be failing or likely to fail to give its pupils an acceptable standard of education, and OFSTED has been informed of this, the registered inspector should:

i   inform the senior managers and the appropriate authority that the judgement of the team is that the school is failing, or likely to fail, to give its pupils an acceptable standard of education, and explain the reasons for this judgement. The following form of words could be used:

'I am of the opinion that special measures are required in relation to this school because it is failing (or is likely to fail) to give its pupils an acceptable standard of education. In accordance with Section 206(2) of the Education Act 1993 I shall send a draft report to HMCI and will await his judgement on whether he agrees or not that this school requires special measures';

ii explain that submission of the draft report to OFSTED may delay the issue of the report to the appropriate authority, but the maximum delay is three months from the time when the report was due; and

iii submit to OFSTED the draft report and such other papers as are required within five weeks of the end of the inspection.

Following receipt of the draft report, HMI from OFSTED will consider the evidence and will usually visit the school before recommending to HMCI whether or not to agree that the school requires special measures.

If HMCI agrees the judgement, the registered inspector must state this in the report and summary of the report. The following form of words should be used:

'In accordance with Section 206(7) of the Education Act 1993[15], I am of the opinion, and HMCI agrees, that special measures are required in relation to this school.'

If HMCI does not agree, OFSTED will discuss available options with the registered inspector.

---

[15] In the case of independent schools (including city technology colleges and city colleges for the technology of the arts) use "In accordance with paragraph 9 of Schedule 2 of the 1992 Education (Schools) Act as amended by paragraph 173 of Schedule 19 to the 1993 Act ..."

PART III

THE INSPECTION SCHEDULE AND GUIDANCE ON ITS USE

THE STRUCTURE OF THE SCHEDULE

■ **This section provides guidance for all inspectors on the use of the inspection schedule which is set out in the *Framework*.** The schedule is the key to producing a report which evaluates the school accurately and informatively.

■ The diagram below shows the structure of the schedule, and hence the inspection report. It highlights the distinction between *outcomes*, with an emphasis on attainment and progress, and the *factors which contribute to these outcomes*, particularly teaching.

CONTEXT				
		3.1 Characteristics of the School		

OUTCOMES				
	4.2		**4.1**	**4.3**
Educational standards achieved	Attitudes, behaviour & personal development		**Attainment & progress**	Attendance

CONTRIBUTORY FACTORS					
	5.2	**5.3**	**5.1**	**5.4**	**5.5**
Provision	The curriculum & assessment	Pupils' spiritual moral, social & cultural development	Teaching	Support, guidance & pupils' welfare	Partnership with parents & the community
	6.2		**6.1**	**6.3**	
Management	Staffing, accommodation & learning resources		Leadership & management	The efficiency of the school	

In using each section of the schedule, inspectors should have regard for what is achieved by and provided for *all* pupils in the school, whatever their age, attainment, gender, background, ethnicity or special educational need.

The inspection findings should be set in the context of the school and its own aims and priorities for development. This background is established in Section 3.1.

OUTCOMES

■ **Educational standards achieved by pupils** are covered in three sections.

◆ *Attainment and progress* focuses on the first priority of inspection: to determine what pupils know, understand and can do, and how this compares with national standards or expectations; and to evaluate their progress.

◆ *Attitudes, behaviour and personal development* constitutes pupils' response to what the school offers through its teaching and other provision.

◆ *Attendance* – including punctuality – reflects another kind of response to school.

Inspection reports should concentrate in these sections on judgements about outcomes, as distinct from the quality of what is provided and other contributory factors.

CONTRIBUTORY FACTORS

■ **Provision, or the quality of education provided,** is covered in five sections, and should be evaluated in terms of its contribution to the outcomes.

◆ *Teaching* is the major factor contributing to pupils' attainment, progress and response. Thorough evaluation of its quality and its impact on the educational standards achieved by pupils is, therefore, central to inspection.

Reporting on the rest of these sections should concentrate on strengths and weaknesses, illustrating the judgements with examples drawn from the evidence base. Where the aspect concerned is satisfactory or unexceptional, only a brief evaluation is needed.

◆ *The curriculum and assessment* involves evaluation of how the school provides and assesses a full range of learning experiences in order to promote the attainment, progress and personal development of all pupils.

◆ *The spiritual, moral, social and cultural development of pupils* is concerned with four aspects of personal development in which schools have an important part to play.

◆ *Support, guidance and pupils' welfare* focuses on the provision the school makes to enable all pupils to take full advantage of the educational opportunities offered, to feel secure and to have high but realistic expectations of themselves.

◆ *Partnership with parents and the community* explores the links which can strengthen the support and guidance of pupils, enrich curricular opportunities and help pupils to progress.

These sections focus on different aspects of provision but are interrelated. They draw largely from the same body of evidence: the school's documentation; the views of parents; observation of work in classrooms and other activities; scrutiny of pupils' work; and discussions with pupils, governors, headteacher and staff.

■ **The management and efficiency of the school** is covered in three sections which are closely connected.

 ◆ *Leadership and management* is concerned with the educational standards set, the quality of provision and the monitoring and evaluation undertaken to promote and sustain their improvement.

 ◆ *Staffing, accommodation and learning resources* is concerned with the adequacy of the school's resources and their impact on standards and quality.

 ◆ *The efficiency of the school* calls for a summative judgement on the use the school makes of its available resources to achieve the best possible outcomes for all its pupils.

SUBJECTS AND COURSES

■ Evaluation of pupils' attainment and progress and the school's provision for the subjects and courses of the curriculum is at the heart of the inspection process. It forms the basis for judging the educational standards of the school and provides much of the evidence about the quality of provision, particularly teaching, as well as the impact of the management and efficiency of the school.

REPORTING

■ Collecting and analysing evidence means that the same issues are often seen from different perspectives. The registered inspector should avoid duplication or repetition when writing the report. One example is assessment, aspects of which relate to teaching, the curriculum and partnership with parents.

■ The **main findings** of the report must highlight educational standards, but they provide the opportunity to show links between outcomes, provision and management. The main findings must incorporate evaluation of the four statutory areas to be reported on, identifying major strengths and weaknesses. The **key issues for action** should draw from the main findings to provide a basis on which the school can act.

THE STRUCTURE OF THE GUIDANCE

■ The sections follow a common pattern. Each page from the *Framework schedule* is matched by *guidance* which includes the following elements.

The **inspection focus** highlights the central judgements which **must** be made. It provides an interpretation of those parts of the schedule which define what inspectors must evaluate and report on. Inspectors must be clear about the judgements to be made to give purpose and direction to the gathering and interpretation of evidence.

Using the criteria illustrates how the criteria should be interpreted and how the evidence is tested against them. The criteria amount to standards for good practice. They provide inspectors with a basis for accurate and consistent evaluation and for the identification of strengths and weaknesses. In reaching overall judgements, all the relevant criteria should be considered.

The criteria can be used in different ways. On the one hand, they can be used to test and check an initial view or hypothesis, for example, that the observed teaching is very good. Alternatively, they can be used cumulatively to build up an overall judgement, for example about the curriculum.

Guidance on using the criteria is provided as a source of reference and not as a prescription to be followed. In using the guidance it is important for the inspection team to focus on the central judgements required by the Framework and not to pursue such a diverse range of issues that the inspection becomes unmanageable.

In reporting, inspectors should avoid simply quoting criteria and should concentrate on the reporting requirements highlighted in the schedule. Evidence needs to be drawn into the report to illustrate judgements, bring the report to life and capture the individual characteristics of the school.

The summary of **main sources of evidence** outlines the key evidence to be collected and analysed before and during the inspection to enable the central judgements to be made.

Additional notes provide guidance where necessary on particular issues covered in the schedule.

Inspection schedule

1 Main Findings

The "Main Findings" (Section 1) together with the "Key Issues for Action" (Section 2) will be included in the summary report which is distributed to parents. These sections must be written in a clear and comprehensible style appropriate for this readership.

THE REPORT MUST INCLUDE

- a summary of the main inspection judgements on the educational standards achieved in the school.

- an evaluation of the school's effectiveness in promoting high standards through the quality of education provided, concentrating in particular upon the quality of teaching, and including the spiritual, moral, social and cultural development of pupils, and the efficiency with which the school's resources are managed.

Where a school is judged to be failing or likely to fail to give its pupils an acceptable standard of education and therefore requires special measures, this must be stated[16].

Where a school has previously been inspected under Section 9 or Section 3(1) of the 1992 Act, the report should give the date of the previous inspection and should summarise the steps taken by the school to implement the action plan which resulted from the inspection.

---

[16] As required by the 1992 Act and amended by Section 206(7) of the 1993 Act.

Guidance on using the schedule

INSPECTION FOCUS

■ The main findings should reflect the essential characteristics and qualities of the school. They should focus on the educational standards achieved by pupils and the strengths and weaknesses in the quality of education provided, especially teaching, and on the management and efficiency of the school as they affect the standards.

The main findings should incorporate summary judgements on the four reporting requirements:

◆ the educational standards achieved by pupils in the school;

◆ the quality of education provided;

◆ the spiritual, moral, social and cultural development of pupils; and

◆ the efficiency with which the financial resources available to the school are managed.

As well as pointing to any significant areas in need of improvement, the opportunity should be taken to highlight what the school does particularly well.

Where a school is judged to be failing, or likely to fail, to give its pupils an acceptable standard of education, this must be stated in the main findings. The form of words which must be used is given in Part II of the *Handbook*.

If a school has previously been inspected under Section 9 or subsequently under Section 3(1) of the 1992 Act, the main findings should conclude with an evaluative comment on the extent to which issues identified in the previous inspection have been dealt with. The summary should state how well the school has responded to the previous inspection, indicating those issues on which significant progress has been made and any outstanding matters which need attention.

2 Key Issues for Action

THE REPORT MUST INCLUDE

■ a list of the specific matters which the appropriate authority for the school must address in constructing its action plan.

The **key issues for action** should draw from the **main findings** and focus on the most significant weaknesses identified in the inspection, particularly in relation to pupils' attainment and progress and the quality of education provided, with particular emphasis on teaching. They are likely to be few in number and should provide a clear and practicable basis on which the appropriate authority and school can act.

Details of any non-compliance with statutory requirements should be included where they detract significantly from the quality and standards of the school together with any significant concerns about health and safety.

The key issues should be given in an order of priority which reflects their importance in improving pupils' attainment. Where the inspection highlights issues already identified as priorities in the school's development plan, this section should make reference to the fact.

Guidance on using the schedule

INSPECTION FOCUS

■ The key issues identified by the inspection will form the basis of the school's action plan. It is important, therefore, that the key issues:

- derive from the main findings;

- are clear, precise and specific to the school;

- provide a practical basis for identifiable improvements in the educational standards achieved by pupils.

The order of priority should reflect the significance of the issues in contributing to the educational standards achieved by pupils, with an emphasis on matters which can realistically be addressed and progress made within, for example, the year following the inspection. This order of priority should be explained during feedback.

There is no need to manufacture these issues in very effective schools where there are no significant weaknesses.

The registered inspector should ensure that the implications of the issues raised are fully understood by the headteacher and governors, and that the issues are expressed unequivocally in the report. For example, "the curriculum needs to be reviewed in mathematics and science" is no substitute for "to raise attainment in mathematics and science at Key Stage 3, pupils' work has to be more challenging."

Mention should also be made of any provision or practice noted during the inspection which, in the opinion of the inspectors, may constitute a significant breach of the law or a serious threat to health and safety. Compliance with statutory requirements is covered in Section 6.1. Guidance on health and safety is given in the commentary on Section 5.4.

Inspection schedule

3 Introduction

3.1 CHARACTERISTICS OF THE SCHOOL

THE REPORT MUST INCLUDE

■ a concise factual statement about the characteristics of the school and its pupils and the area it serves.

The statement should include the number of pupils on roll, the number of pupils identified as having special educational needs and a description of the composition of the school in terms of pupils' attainment on entry, gender, ethnicity and background.

■ a brief statement of the main aims and priorities of the school, including any targets set by the school.

The text of section 3.1 should be agreed with the headteacher and the appropriate authority.

Guidance on using the schedule

INSPECTION FOCUS

■ This section should briefly describe the school in a way which provides relevant information as a background to the inspection report, limited where possible to two paragraphs.

The first paragraph should state the characteristics listed in the inspection schedule. The registered inspector and the appropriate authority may, however, agree to include in this paragraph other features which are significant to the inspection, for example, a recent large change in roll. The main sources of evidence are the PICSI report, the *Headteacher's Form* and *Statement* and the discussion which takes place with the headteacher and appropriate authority.

The second paragraph should capture what the school sees as its main aims and priorities. Particular mention should be made of any targets, related to educational standards, which the school has set. The school's aims and priorities will be drawn from the prospectus, the school development plan and from discussion.

It is particularly important to ensure that the headteacher and appropriate authority agree that the second paragraph reflects accurately the school's main aims, priorities and targets.

Evaluation of the relevance of the aims, priorities and targets, and of how they have been pursued, should be reported in Section 6.1.

In a PRU, the statement should include the number of pupils re-integrated into secondary schools in the past year.

Inspection schedule

3.2 KEY INDICATORS

THE REPORT MUST INCLUDE

■ The report should include the key indicators which summarise the attainment of pupils at the end of each key stage and at 17 and 18 years, together with national comparative data where these are available.

Depending on the time of the inspection, national data may or may not refer to the same school year. The years to which the data refer should be clearly stated.

At the end of Key Stage 2 (in middle deemed secondary schools):

Proportion of pupils attaining level 4 or above in specified subjects or attainment targets.

At the end of Key Stage 3:

Proportion of pupils attaining levels 5 and above, and 6 and above, in specified subjects or attainment targets.

At the end of Key Stage 4 and in the sixth form:

Comparative attainment data from the annual performance tables.

■ The report should include school and comparative national attendance data, showing the percentages of half days missed through authorised and through unauthorised absence.

School exclusion data should show the numbers of fixed term and permanent exclusions of pupils of compulsory school age during the previous school year.

OFSTED will from time to time provide registered inspectors and contractors with a current specification of data to be included in the report.

■ The report should also state the percentage of teaching observed in the school as a whole which was: very good or better; satisfactory or better; and less than satisfactory.

Guidance on using the schedule

INSPECTION FOCUS

■ **The report should present the school's data clearly and concisely, alongside comparative data provided by OFSTED.** The format of presentation is, however, left to the registered inspector, whose aim should be to make the data as clear as possible to a lay readership.

The National Curriculum assessment and test data required from schools is drawn from that which is published for parents. The registered inspector is responsible for compiling this data as specified for the report. The KS4 and sixth form attainment data prescribed for the report are those required for publication in the annual performance tables. Other data for this section of the report can be taken directly from the *Headteacher's Form*.

The data on the proportion of teaching which is very good or better, satisfactory or better, and less than satisfactory should be compiled from the observation of teaching. Very good teaching is summarised as grades 1 and 2 on the 7-point scale; satisfactory or better as grades 1 to 4; and less than satisfactory as grades 5 to 7.

Details of the grading scale are given in the *Inspection Resource Pack*.

PRUs are not required to comply with the arrangements for National Curriculum assessment and testing.

Inspection schedule

PART A: ASPECTS OF THE SCHOOL

4 Educational standards achieved by pupils at the school

4.1 ATTAINMENT AND PROGRESS

Inspectors must evaluate and report on what pupils achieve by the end of each key stage, and by 19 with reference, where appropriate, to:

■ attainment;

i   in the school overall, in relation to national standards or expectations including National Targets for Education and Training, where appropriate, highlighting any significant variations in attainment among pupils of different gender, ethnicity or background;

ii   in English, mathematics and science, and in the other subjects or areas inspected, highlighting relative strengths and weaknesses;

iii   over time, if there are any clear trends in overall attainment, with a comment on how well any targets set or adopted by the school are being met.

■ progress in relation to prior attainment.

Judgements should be based on the extent to which:

◆ the attainment of pupils at 11, 14 and 16 years meets or exceeds national standards, particularly in English, mathematics and science;

◆ students by 19 years achieve or exceed two GCE A-level passes or equivalent[17] and leave school with qualifications relevant to the next stage of education or training, or employment;

◆ high, average and low attaining pupils, including those with special educational needs, progress as well as or better than expected;

◆ the attainment and progress of minority groups of pupils is comparable with others in the school;

◆ the school sustains high levels of attainment or is improving.

---

17   For example, advanced GNVQ.

Guidance on using the schedule

INSPECTION FOCUS

■ The main priorities of inspection are to *assess* what pupils know, understand and can do (their attainment), and to *evaluate* their progress.

Inspectors must report, firstly, on how the attainment of pupils at each stage of education compares with national averages in terms of results in key stage tests and assessments and external examinations, or, where these are not available, expectations for the age group concerned. This, therefore, is an age-related judgement which should not make allowance for pupils' perceived potential or ability.

Overall judgements must focus:

◆ at KS2 (for middle schools) and KS3, on outcomes in the core subjects and evidence of attainment in all the subjects inspected;

◆ at KS4 and post-16, on examination results and other accreditation and evidence of attainment in all subjects inspected.

The report should provide a short commentary which interprets National Curriculum and examination results in the light of evidence of attainment gathered in the inspection.

The report should also comment on comparative attainment between subjects.

The second judgement is concerned with whether, given their current levels of attainment, pupils are making – and have made – significant progress. This calls on inspectors to gather and evaluate a complex set of evidence which ranges from progress observed in lessons, (i.e. 'what did pupils learn?'), to progress over longer periods of time and from one stage of schooling to the next. Progress is defined as gains in knowledge, understanding and skill.

Inspectors should analyse and report on any significant differences in the attainment and progress made by different groups of pupils. The report should comment specifically on the progress of pupils with special educational need. In PRUs, inspectors should take account of progress towards re-integration.

USING THE CRITERIA

Does the attainment of pupils at 11 (in middle schools), 14 and 16 years meet or exceed national standards, particularly in English, mathematics and science?

■ The emphasis on English, mathematics and science reflects the importance of these core subjects in the National Curriculum. Judgements at KS2 (in middle schools) and KS3 should take into account the school's results in both tests and teacher assessments. These must be set in the context of national comparative data, interpretation of which will develop over time and will be communicated by OFSTED. At KS4, judgements of attainment should take into account performance in all GCSE or other examinations, setting this in the context of national figures.

Guidance on using the schedule

However, at both KS3 and KS4, inspectors need to go beyond test and examination results, which invariably apply to pupils who have moved into a new year group or who may have left the school. These results do not give the complete picture. Inspectors need to judge, therefore, how the attainment of pupils at the time of the inspection relates to what is expected, on average, for the year group, using their expertise alongside National Curriculum level descriptions and the requirements of GCSE or other accreditation as points of reference.

In relation to English and mathematics, inspectors should draw on evidence from across the curriculum. The report should make it clear whether the essential skills of these subjects, i.e. reading, writing, speaking, listening and the use of number, are sufficiently developed to enhance learning across the curriculum or whether the levels of such skills are too low and are a barrier to progress.

Inspectors should report strengths and weaknesses in the attainment of pupils at 11 (in middle schools), 14 and 16 in the other subjects or courses inspected. Evidence should include pupils' work, discussion and observation. This will be especially important in those subjects or courses for which test and examination data is limited or unavailable. In these cases, inspectors should base their judgements on their knowledge of the average range of attainment for pupils at these ages. Inspectors in PRUs may not be able to draw on end-of-key stage results.

Do students by 19 years achieve or exceed two GCE A-level passes or the equivalent and leave school with qualifications relevant to the next stage of education or training?

■ Attainment by students post-16 should be judged taking account of the criteria, including the grade or performance criteria, for the course being followed. Inspectors should use national average grades, point scores or pass rates for the subjects or courses concerned, to set the performance of students in the school in context. They should take account of the difference in assessment regimes between vocational courses such as GNVQ, which are criterion-referenced, and other examinations with aggregated forms of assessment, such as GCSE and A/AS-level. Inspectors should also take account of the destinations of school leavers.

There are some general features of attainment post-16 which can be used to guide evaluation across a range of courses:

♦ a secure grasp of relevant specialist knowledge and its application;

♦ the development of intellectual skills and a capacity to be innovative in their use;

♦ higher-level experimental and investigational skills;

♦ the ability to analyse, interpret and critically evaluate material from a variety of sources;

♦ the ability to construct and express, both orally and in writing, relevant, coherent and cogent explanation and argument;

♦ the ability to interpret data in a variety of forms and, when appropriate, make predictions or formulate hypotheses and test them;

♦ the development of individual strategies for the management and completion of tasks, in preparation for effective progression to continuing education, training or employment.

Do high, average and low attaining pupils, including those with special education needs, progress as well as or better than expected?

Is the attainment and progress of minority groups comparable with others in the school?

■ These two criteria call for evaluation of the progress pupils make: their *gains* in knowledge, understanding and skills. Analysis depends on comparing current with prior attainment.

It is possible for pupils having above-average attainment to make unsatisfactory progress because it is not as good as expected in relation to their prior attainment. Conversely, pupils with very low attainment may make better than expected progress even though eventual attainment still falls short of the average for their age.

Evidence of progress should come from the following sources:

◆ observation of pupils at work provides evidence of new learning or of consolidation or application of knowledge, understanding and skills over a short timescale – that is, within a lesson or sequence of lessons;

◆ records from primary or middle schools – sometimes accompanied by samples of work – should indicate the attainment of pupils on entry in some or all of the National Curriculum subjects;

◆ the outcomes of KS2 tests and teacher assessments, and in middle schools to KS1, as these become available;

◆ results of standardised tests on entry (where schools use these for diagnostic or screening purposes) may provide useful evidence, for example in relation to reading;

◆ samples of pupils' earlier work should be reviewed in the light of current work to assess progress made;

◆ progress in Key Stage 4 can be checked against the results of KS3 tests and teacher assessments;

◆ progression of post-16 students through the subject or course can be traced in relation to earlier GCSE or other examination performance, and some schools will be in a position to provide a detailed analysis of their progress through the accreditation system;

◆ reference to teachers' individual records, pupil records (including records of achievement) and reports to parents can together give a detailed picture of prior attainment, targets for improvement and progress made;

◆ for pupils with special educational needs, detailed information on the prior attainment, targets for improvement and progress made can be gained from individual education plans, statements and annual reviews;

◆ discussion with pupils about what they are doing now, what they have learned or what they are going on to do next can be illuminating.

It is important to examine the progress of different groups of pupils – for example, the different sexes, or pupils from minority ethnic backgrounds. Some schools provide more effectively for some groups than for others and inspectors need to highlight significant variations and the reasons for them. Inspectors should enquire into whether the school monitors the performance of different groups and, if so, what the data reveals and how the school responds.

Guidance on using the schedule

In PRUs, inspectors should evaluate the progress made by pupils since entry to the PRU in relation both to previous attainment and length of time in the unit.

Is the school sustaining high standards or improving?

■ Evidence of markedly high standards, or sustained improvement or decline over several years, should be reported. Such evidence should be treated cautiously where the size of groups or entries for particular examinations reduces statistical reliability. A judgement should only be made where there is solid evidence of a trend in performance, up or down, over three or four years.

Some schools set quantitative targets for improvement at school, key stage or subject level and monitor progress towards such targets. Inspectors should consider whether the targets set are appropriate and achievable, and how well they are met.

Some schools may have adopted local targets or the National Targets for Education and Training, details of which are given below.

The National Targets for Education and Training for 2000 are:

i   by the age of 19, 85% of young people to achieve 5 GCSEs at grade C or above, an intermediate GNVQ or an NVQ level 2;

ii   75% of young people to achieve level 2 competence in communication, numeracy and IT by age 19 (and 35% to achieve level 3 competence in these core skills by age 21);

iii by age 21, 60% of young people to achieve 2 GCE A-levels, an Advanced GNVQ or an NVQ level 3.

MAIN SOURCES OF EVIDENCE

Before the inspection

◆ **National Curriculum assessments,** both test results and teacher assessment;

◆ **the PICSI report** gives comparative data;

◆ **evidence of attainment** provided by the school should give a picture of the level and distribution of attainment for pupils who were at the end of a key stage or in the sixth form in the summer before the inspection; and, for PRUs, previous school records and reports issued on entry to the PRU.

During the inspection

The team should gather evidence of the current and past attainment of pupils throughout the school. While particular attention should be given to what is attained by pupils by the end of middle schools, and those aged 14, 16 and above in secondary schools, it is important to assess attainment in all years to see whether progress is greater or less at particular ages. Evidence includes:

◆ **teacher assessments, pupils' records** and their current and earlier work. In some schools the evidence may also include information such as the results of standardised tests on entry to the school or a "value-added" analysis of the progress made by pupils in a year group based on prior attainment data;

◆ **analysis of statements, individual education plans and annual reviews** for a sample of pupils on the school's register of special educational needs; evidence of progress for pupils for whom English not the home language;

◆ **observation of pupils at work;**

◆ **discussion with a sample of high, average and low-attaining pupils** provides valuable insights about their knowledge and understanding of their work in hand and progress they have made.

Inspection schedule

4.2 ATTITUDES, BEHAVIOUR AND PERSONAL DEVELOPMENT

Inspectors must evaluate and report on pupils' response to the teaching and other provision made by the school, highlighting strengths and weaknesses, as shown by:

■ their attitudes to learning;

■ their behaviour, including incidence of exclusions;

■ the quality of relationships in the school including the degree of racial harmony, where applicable;

■ other aspects of their personal development, including their contributions to the life of the community.

Judgements should be based on the extent to which pupils:

◆ show interest in their work and are able to sustain concentration and develop their capacity for personal study;

◆ behave well in and around the school, and are courteous and trustworthy and show respect for property;

◆ form constructive relationships with one another, with teachers and other adults, and work collaboratively when required;

◆ show respect for other people's feelings, values and beliefs;

◆ show initiative and are willing to take responsibility.

Guidance on using the schedule

INSPECTION FOCUS

■ This section is concerned with how pupils respond to the school in terms of their attitudes to learning, their behaviour and their values and personal development. The criteria here cover pupils' response to the school's provision, particularly teaching, the curriculum and the provision for spiritual, moral, social and cultural development.

■ Pupils' attitudes have a significant bearing on their attainment and progress and can be strongly influenced by what schools do. Good behaviour is vital to productive learning, the quality of life in the school and to the functioning of the school as an orderly community.

Definitions of aspects of personal development are given in Section 5.3. What is at issue here is the development of individual values and beliefs and the maturity of the pupils' response to experiences which broaden their understanding of their own and other people's lives.

■ Overall judgements should identify strengths and weaknesses in pupils' attitudes to learning and any variations for particular groups of pupils. On the basis of the team's observations in lessons and around the school, inspectors should judge pupils' behaviour and its effect on their learning and on the school. Where there are strengths or weaknesses in behaviour and relationships these should be stated. A judgement should also be made on the basis of all the evidence available about the overall quality of pupils' personal development.

Pupils in PRUs have usually experienced significant difficulties in behaviour and motivation before entering the unit. Inspectors should look for the development, from a low baseline, of positive attitudes to learning, good behaviour and personal responsibility.

USING THE CRITERIA

Do pupils show interest in their work? Are they able to sustain concentration and extend their capacity for personal study?

■ Inspectors should look for evidence of pupils' involvement in and enjoyment of learning, their willingness to apply themselves to the task in hand, respond to challenging tasks, to learn from mistakes, to ask and answer questions, to join in discussion and show enthusiasm.

Important evidence should emerge from discussion with pupils about whether they enjoy their work, what they find easy or difficult; how they tackle new work and what they think of their contributions in lessons.

A positive approach to work is shown in:

◆   their concentration in listening to the teacher;

◆   how confidently pupils work independently to generate ideas and solve problems;

◆   their capacity to persevere and complete tasks when difficulties arise;

◆ their ability to select and use relevant resources;

◆ their desire to improve their work and their pride in the finished product.

There should be evidence of older pupils and students carrying more responsibility for the organisation of their work, taking the initiative and setting some of their own tasks in discussion with their teachers.

How well do pupils behave in and around the school? Are they courteous and trustworthy? Do they show respect for property?

Do pupils form constructive relationships with one another, with teachers and other adults and work collaboratively when required?

■ Most of the evidence from which to judge behaviour and relationships in the school will be derived from observation in and outside lessons. Evidence collected in relation to Section 5.1 will be central. The analysis should also take into account the views of the headteacher, staff, governors, pupils and parents. In particular, the meeting with parents should explore their perceptions of behaviour, the information they receive about rewards and sanctions and the extent to which their children are happy and confident at school.

In classrooms the main issue is whether pupils' behaviour helps their learning or obstructs it. Outside classrooms inspectors should observe how well pupils respond to the school's rules and conventions. There are significant weaknesses in behaviour when teachers or support staff spend an undue amount of time seeking to establish and maintain order.

Inspectors need to observe pupils and talk to them and to staff to see whether there is any inappropriate behaviour. Observation of behaviour and discussion with pupils and teachers will show the extent to which pupils know right from wrong and take responsibility for their own actions.

Inspectors should look for evidence of:

◆ the ways in which pupils, including those of different ethnic groups, relate to one another;

◆ any inappropriate behaviour, including harassment or bullying, by or towards particular groups of pupils;

◆ pupils' ability to work together in lessons and to support one another in other school activities;

◆ the level of respect between pupils and teachers and other adults in school, and whether pupils are encouraged to articulate their own views and beliefs;

◆ pupils' and students' behaviour off the school site, in, for example, work experience placements;

◆ the way pupils treat the school's and other people's property.

The number of, and the reasons for, exclusions from the school, both permanent and fixed-term, should be considered. The PICSI report gives comparative data. Inspectors should establish whether correct procedures are followed, whether exclusions are monitored with regard to gender and ethnicity and what patterns emerge.

In a PRU, inspectors should evaluate the extent to which pupils behave in a socially acceptable manner, improve their concentration and engage in their programme of work.

Do pupils show respect for other people's feelings, values and beliefs?

■ Evidence comes from observation of pupils at work, at play, and in other school activities and from discussion with pupils and staff. It includes:

◆ pupils' perceptiveness, their willingness to listen to what others in the school have to say and their interest in views and ideas different from their own;

◆ their recognition and increasing understanding of the diversity of beliefs, attitudes, and social and cultural traditions;

◆ their capacity to reflect on and discuss their behaviour, feelings and experiences.

Do pupils show initiative and are they willing to take responsibility?

■ This entails looking at pupils' involvement in the daily routines of the school, their response to teaching and the curriculum, and their participation in activities which link with the wider community. Inspectors should observe whether pupils offer to help; whether they see what needs to be done; whether they help to organise other pupils; whether they have particular responsibilities in the school or in the classroom. Inspectors should consider if there is increasing scope for pupils to take responsibility and show initiative as they move up the school, or, in a PRU, as they prepare to re-integrate into school.

Evidence may come from discussion with staff and from talking to a sample of pupils in particular year groups. The key is how pupils respond to the opportunities offered – for example, in presenting assemblies, putting on performances, running clubs, taking part in charitable events, arranging activities for community groups, helping in the library or the IT centre, being involved in mini-enterprises, helping to supervise younger pupils, working with them on their reading – and so on.

Guidance on using the schedule

MAIN SOURCES OF EVIDENCE

Before the inspection

◆ **the prospectus, staff handbook and behaviour and discipline policy** may set out particular strategies to encourage positive attitudes and personal development;

◆ **discussion at pre-inspection meetings** with the headteacher, governors and parents, and scrutiny of the completed parents' questionnaire provide a range of perspectives on pupils' response to school.

During the inspection

A view on how pupils respond, behave and develop can be gained through:

◆ **observation of pupils in class and around the school**; their participation in extra-curricular activities and contribution to the life of the school; interaction between pupils and staff;

◆ **discussion with pupils, teaching and support staff** exploring the extent to which the school promotes positive attitudes;

◆ **scrutiny of records** of behaviour and sanctions, including exclusions, and analysis of the nature and patterns of any poor behaviour.

Inspection schedule

4.3 ATTENDANCE

INSPECTORS MUST EVALUATE AND REPORT ON

- ■ pupils' attendance and punctuality, analysing reasons for absence where attendance is poor or where patterns of absence affect particular groups of pupils.

Judgements should be based on the extent to which:

- ◆ pupils' attendance exceeds 90% and they come to school and lessons on time.

Guidance on using the schedule

INSPECTION FOCUS

■ Evaluation should focus on the level of pupils' attendance and its effect on attainment and progress. Section 5.4 covers the action that the school takes.

■ Attendance of the great majority of pupils will be regular, but in some schools there are high levels of intermittent and extended absence, much of it unauthorised. Internal truancy may also be a feature in some schools. For some pupils attendance may be interrupted by long periods of illness or medical treatment.

Attendance by students over 16 is not required by law but a school with a sixth form should have a policy on attendance for students who are registered. The policy should include the use of independent study time.

■ The overall judgement should indicate any significant features of pupils' attendance and punctuality and comment on the effect on their attainment and progress.

USING THE CRITERIA

Does pupils' attendance exceed 90% and do they come to school and lessons on time?

■ Where attendance for the whole school or for year groups falls below 90% or where there are indications of significant internal truancy or poor punctuality, an analysis of patterns of absence and their effect on attainment and progress needs to be undertaken. This analysis may show whether poor attendance or punctuality affects particular groups of pupils. Discussion with staff and the school's education welfare officer may help to illuminate the patterns and causes of absence.

In a PRU individual rates of attendance may vary. Some pupils may attend on a part-time basis, in which case attendance is judged in relation to the possible maximum. There should be a plan for increasing the attendance of individual pupils with poor attendance.

Guidance on using the schedule

MAIN SOURCES OF EVIDENCE

Before the inspection

◆ the *Headteacher's Form* provides data on pupils' attendance;

◆ the PICSI report compares data with schools of similar character nationally;

◆ **parents' views** should be sought at the pre-inspection meeting;

During the inspection

◆ **scrutiny of registers** will confirm compliance with statutory requirements and allow inspectors to assess any significant patterns of absence, and **registration periods** should be sampled;

◆ **lesson observation** will provide a comparison of the number of pupils present with the number listed for the class; any delays or disruption caused by lateness should be noted;

◆ **discussions with staff, the welfare officer and pupils** should explore the extent to which attendance and punctuality affects teaching, attainment and progress.

◆ **scrutiny of school policies** may provide insights into the policy on sixth form attendance; the day-to-day management of attendance issues; and planned strategies to support individual pupils on their return from a period of extended absence.

Inspection schedule

5 Quality of education provided

5.1 TEACHING

INSPECTORS MUST EVALUATE AND REPORT ON

■ the quality of teaching and its contribution to pupils' attainment and progress, highlighting:

i overall strengths and weaknesses in teaching pupils in each key stage, in the sixth form and in the different subjects or areas of learning inspected;

ii factors which account for effective and ineffective teaching;

iii the extent to which teaching meets the needs of all pupils, paying particular attention to any pupils who have special educational needs or for whom English is an additional language.

Judgements should be based on the extent to which teachers[18]:

◆ have a secure knowledge and understanding of the subjects or areas they teach;

◆ set high expectations so as to challenge pupils and deepen their knowledge and understanding;

◆ plan effectively;

◆ employ methods and organisational strategies which match curricular objectives and the needs of all pupils;

◆ manage pupils well and achieve high standards of discipline;

◆ use time and resources effectively;

◆ assess pupils' work thoroughly and constructively, and use assessments to inform teaching;

◆ use homework effectively to reinforce and/or extend what is learned in school.

---

[18] Or other staff involved in teaching, instruction or providing support for learning.

Guidance on using the schedule

INSPECTION FOCUS

- Teaching is the major factor contributing to pupils' attainment, progress and response. Evaluation of the quality and impact of teaching is central to inspection. Assessment is integral to the teaching process; this section covers teachers' formative day-to-day assessment, while Section 5.2 deals with the school's arrangements for assessment and recording and Section 5.5 with reporting to parents.

- In secondary schools most subject teaching is undertaken by specialist teachers working with pupils or students grouped on the basis of attainment, age or stage in a course. Teachers' command of the subject and the teaching methods and strategies they employ should be appropriate to the relevant key stage or course and the needs of pupils.

- Overall judgements about teaching will derive from those made in each lesson observed, covering the subjects inspected and all year groups in the school. Pupils' work provides supplementary evidence. The report should include illustrations of successful and less successful teaching methods.

USING THE CRITERIA

Do teachers have a secure knowledge and understanding of the subjects or areas they teach?

- The assessment of teachers' subject expertise begins with their knowledge and understanding of the subjects and courses they teach. This includes, where appropriate, familiarity with the National Curriculum subject Orders, the relevant RE syllabus and course and examination requirements. In the case of vocational courses, teachers need knowledge and experience of general vocational requirements, core skills, assessment methods and the relevant industrial, commercial or services sector.

Records of qualifications, experience and training will be a starting point but the main sources of evidence will be observation of teaching, supported by study of teachers' planning and discussion with them.

Inspectors can judge teachers' subject knowledge by observing, for example, their:

- ◆ competence in teaching the content of the National Curriculum programmes of study and the RE syllabus, examination and vocational courses;

- ◆ competence in planning activities and carrying them out;

- ◆ skill in asking relevant questions and providing explanations;

- ◆ perceptiveness in marking and responding to pupils' work;

- ability to draw on a range of contexts and resources to make subject knowledge comprehensible to pupils;

- success in providing demanding work for the more able pupils.

Do teachers set high expectations so as to challenge pupils and deepen their knowledge and understanding?

■ Inspectors need to identify the level of challenge in the content, activities and learning resources provided for pupils of different attainment. They should evaluate whether the teaching is well matched to the pupils' stage of learning and moves them on.

Teachers' expectations of pupils relate closely to their knowledge of the subjects or courses they teach, their knowledge of what pupils have already achieved, and their understanding of how pupils will gain most from the teaching. Good teaching makes clear the importance of application, accuracy and good presentation, and the need to use critical thinking, creativity and imagination. It provides the stimulus, the knowledge and the methods for pupils to do their best in all these respects. Teaching should provide opportunities for students to take increasing responsibility for their own work.

Expectations may be set too low; they can also be pitched unrealistically high if pupils are not ready for the task or do not have adequate resources, support or time to undertake it effectively.

Do teachers plan effectively?

■ Good planning means that the teaching in a lesson or a sequence of lessons has clear objectives for what pupils are to learn and how these objectives will be achieved. It will take account of the differing needs of pupils. Plans can take a number of forms; for example, schemes of work may include detailed lesson plans, but these may be separate. Whatever form planning takes, inspectors need to look for evidence of teaching intentions and how they will be met. They should look for evidence that planning:

- incorporates National Curriculum programmes of study, syllabus and course requirements;

- sets out clear objectives;

- summarises what pupils will do and the resources they will need;

- shows how knowledge and understanding can be extended, and the work adapted to suit pupils who learn at different rates;

- in PRUs, assists pupils' re-integration into school.

Where possible, inspectors should discuss with teachers the context of lessons, how the lesson fits into a longer-term plan and why, for example, particular methods are used. Such discussion provides insight into teachers' planning and their response to changing situations which are not always recorded on paper.

In some classes inspectors will need to consider how support staff are used and how they are informed about teaching and learning objectives and involved in planning.

Do teachers employ methods and organisational strategies which match curricular objectives and the needs of all pupils?

■ The choice of teaching methods and organisational strategies is a matter for the school and the teacher's discretion. It should take into account the objectives of the lesson and factors such as the number of pupils, their age, attainment and behaviour, and the nature of the resources and accommodation.

The key to the judgement is whether the methods and organisation are fit for the purpose of achieving high standards of work and behaviour. Direct evidence will come from lesson observation. Scrutiny of pupils' work and discussion with teachers and pupils gives evidence over a longer timescale of whether methods and organisation are sufficiently responsive to the range of curricular objectives and pupils' needs.

Teaching methods include exposition, explanation, demonstration, discussion, practical activity, investigation, testing and problem-solving. The test of their effectiveness is the extent to which they extend or deepen pupils' knowledge and understanding and develop their skills. They are likely to do so when they are selected and handled with careful regard to:

◆ the nature of the curricular objectives being pursued; and

◆ what pupils know, understand and can do, and what they need to learn next.

This test applies to the range of methods – from sustained exposition by the teacher on, for example, an aspect of history to the use of practical work in art. In each case inspectors should consider, for example, whether:

◆ exposition or explanation by the teacher is informative, lively and well structured;

◆ the teacher's use of questions probes pupils' knowledge and understanding and challenges their thinking;

◆ practical activity is purposeful in that pupils are encouraged to think about what they are doing, what they have learned from it and how to improve their work;

◆ investigations and problem-solving activities are efficient in helping pupils to apply and extend their learning in new contexts.

Key issues with regard to how pupils are organised in the class are:

◆ whether the objectives are best achieved by pupils working alone, in pairs or small groups, or all together;

◆ whether the form of organisation allows the teacher to interact with pupils positively and economically.

Good teaching will employ different organisational strategies to pursue different curricular objectives.

In relation to whole class teaching inspectors should consider how well the teacher manages explanation, questioning and discussion so that all pupils are involved and stimulated. In observing group and individual work inspectors should look at how the teacher interacts with pupils to challenge their thinking and keep the work focused and moving at pace. Inspectors should identify whether the teacher is using his or her teaching skills rather than merely servicing the tasks. This is a particular issue when classroom activities cover a number of subjects and use a wide range of resources.

Guidance on using the schedule

In any form of organisation inspectors must consider the effectiveness of the strategies used for supporting pupils with special educational needs and, where relevant, pupils for whom English is an additional language. In observing whole class or group work inspectors also need to be alert to how teachers make sure that all pupils participate and how they handle situations where individuals dominate or are passive.

Do teachers manage pupils well and achieve high standards of discipline?

Do teachers use time and resources effectively?

■ Central to the judgements relating to these criteria is the extent to which the management of pupils' time and resources contributes to pupils working productively – that is, spending a high proportion of the available time 'on task'.

A key point is whether the structuring and the pace of work help sustained learning to take place. In effective lessons or sessions the pace is usually brisk, but there are occasions which need time for reflection and consolidation, or for steady and careful pursuit of a task. Inspectors should judge whether:

◆ the structure of the lesson means that time is well used;

◆ pupils are clear about what they are doing, why they are doing it, how long they have to do it, and the way in which they can judge success in their work.

Taken together, these features are likely to motivate pupils and promote good behaviour.

Vocational courses in KS4 and post-16 put considerable emphasis on assignments. Teachers need to be aware of the impact that such tasks can have on pupils' other work and their management of time.

A judgement is needed about whether resources are appropriately chosen to advance pupils' learning. Resources include reference and other information materials; they may also include special equipment for pupils with disabilities. Some resources used may be outside the classroom – for example, reference material and IT equipment in a library or resource centre. Where possible, inspectors should evaluate the learning that occurs in these circumstances.

Do teachers assess pupils' work thoroughly and constructively, and use assessments to inform teaching?

■ Judgements about assessment should focus on how the day-to-day interventions with pupils, including the marking of work, are used to help pupils to understand what they need to do to improve their work and make progress.

Clues to the effectiveness of formative assessment are how well teachers listen and respond to pupils, encourage and, where appropriate, praise them, recognise and handle their misconceptions, build on their responses and steer them towards new learning or clearer understanding. Interactions of this kind play an important part in the support and encouragement of pupils and may be seen in a variety of contexts including whole class lessons, group work and in individual tasks.

Scrutiny of pupils' books and discussion with pupils provide evidence of the quality of marking, how thoroughly problems are diagnosed, whether comments both encourage and challenge and whether the approaches to marking are consistent. It will be evident in written work whether feedback is having a positive effect.

Particular attention should be paid to how assessment of the work of pupils with special educational needs relates to targets set in individual education plans.

Do teachers use homework effectively to reinforce and/or extend what is learnt in schools?

■ Homework offers opportunities to enhance the quality of work. Inspectors should consider the extent to which staff and pupils take homework seriously, devote the time in lessons to those activities which require direct teaching and set complementary homework, following it up effectively. Doing so allows more productive use to be made of lesson time, extends coverage of the curriculum and improves pupils' study skills.

A carefully planned school approach to homework can build up pupils' capacity to work independently. Evidence of the effectiveness of this approach should be seen, particularly in coursework assignments in KS4 and post-16.

Guidance on using the schedule

MAIN SOURCES OF EVIDENCE

Before the inspection

◆ the *Headteacher's Form and Statement* provide a preliminary view of staff qualifications, training, expertise and experience;

◆ **the staff handbook** (if available) may include a policy for teaching;

◆ **schemes of work, departmental/course handbooks and teachers' planning documents** should show how teachers plan, organise and adapt their teaching to meet the differing needs of pupils;

◆ **assessment policies** may indicate how day-to-day formative assessment is intended to help pupils' progress;

◆ where the school has carried out a review of its teaching, **a scrutiny of school self-review** documentation provides supplementary evidence;

◆ **the pre-inspection meeting with parents** provides an indication of their satisfaction with the overall quality of teaching in the school;

During the inspection

◆ **observation of lessons** should focus on the effect of teaching, on what pupils learn and on their attainment, progress and response;

◆ **a scrutiny of pupils' work** and how it is marked;

◆ **discussion with teachers, support staff and pupils** may provide insight into the extent to which the teaching sets high expectations and promotes the learning of all pupils.

Guidance on using the schedule

ADDITIONAL NOTES

TRAINEE TEACHERS

Where trainee teachers are taking a class during the inspection, the class should be inspected using the same criteria used to judge other teaching in the school. Section 9 inspections should not evaluate school-based elements of initial teacher training, but should comment on the school's participation in training teachers and in particular on the benefits to standards and quality in the school.

SUPPLY TEACHERS

Teaching by supply teachers is part of the provision made by the school and should be inspected as such. Supply teachers will not necessarily have close knowledge of the pupils. The quality of the teaching they offer may be affected by the quality of the information they have been given about the work the class has been doing and should be doing and by whether they are expected to teach a one-off lesson, with or without materials provided. Where the incidence of supply teaching is significant, inspectors should note whether it has a bearing on the quality of provision and on pupils' attainment and progress.

5.2 THE CURRICULUM AND ASSESSMENT

INSPECTORS MUST EVALUATE AND REPORT ON STRENGTHS AND WEAKNESSES IN

■ the planning and content of the curriculum and its contribution to the educational standards achieved by all pupils, taking account of their age, capability, gender, ethnicity, background and special educational need, including reference to:

i the subjects and courses provided to 16, and the post-16 curriculum;

ii the provision made for personal and social education, including health education, sex education where appropriate, and attention to drug misuse;

iii careers education and guidance in schools providing for the secondary age range;

iv extra-curricular activities, including sport;

■ procedures for assessing pupils' attainment.

Judgements should be based on the extent to which the curriculum:

◆ is balanced and broadly based, promotes pupils' intellectual, physical and personal development and prepares pupils for the next stage of education, training, or employment;

◆ meets statutory requirements to teach the subjects of the National Curriculum, religious education and sex education, where these apply;

◆ provides equality of access and opportunity for pupils to learn and to make progress;

◆ meets the curricular requirements of all pupils on the school's Code of Practice special educational needs register;

◆ is planned effectively, providing continuity and progression of learning;

◆ is enriched by extra-curricular provision, including sport;

◆ includes, for pupils of secondary age, careers education and impartial guidance, drawing on the careers service.

and, in relation to assessment, the extent to which:

◆ there are effective systems for assessing pupils' attainment;

◆ assessment information is used to inform curriculum planning.

Guidance on using the schedule

INSPECTION FOCUS

■ Inspection centres on the extent to which the content and organisation of the curriculum and its assessment provide access to the full range of learning experiences and promote the attainment, progress and personal development of all pupils. The curriculum comprises all the planned activities within and beyond the timetable.

■ The curriculum for a maintained middle or secondary school complies with the law if it:

◆ is balanced and broadly based;

◆ promotes the spiritual, moral, cultural, mental and physical development of pupils;

◆ prepares pupils for the opportunities, responsibilities and experiences of adult life;

◆ includes the subjects of the National Curriculum as prescribed in regulations;

◆ provides for religious education in accordance with an agreed syllabus or the school's trust deeds;

◆ provides for sex education in accordance with the school's policy.

Schools should also provide careers education and guidance, and health education, including education about drug misuse.

The school's practice on assessment needs to be seen in relation to:

◆ the assessment requirements of the National Curriculum at the end of KS2 (for middle schools) and KS3;

◆ public examination requirements at KS4 and post-16;

◆ the requirements covering pupil records and reports, including annual reports to parents and reports to school leavers;

◆ the additional requirements which apply to pupils with statements of special educational needs and those at stage 2 or above in the Code of Practice.

The curriculum in secondary schools is usually organised into separate subjects taught by specialist teachers, but other forms of organisation may be used, for example in relation to vocational courses. Provision for curricular elements such as IT and health education may be organised in a variety of ways.

In most schools KS4 provides the first opportunity for pupils to exercise choice over their curriculum and may feature different types of provision for different groups of pupils as permitted by the Dearing review of the National Curriculum.

The curriculum for part-time pupils in PRUs should also comply with Section 1 of the 1988 Education Reform Act.

Many subjects and courses contain elements of **vocational education** which, if fully exploited, contribute to preparing pupils for adult life. Schools may also provide vocational elements such as work experience or other links with business. Nationally accredited vocational courses may also be offered at KS4 and post-16. Several vocational awarding bodies offer awards which lead to General National Vocational Qualifications (GNVQs) or to National Vocational Qualifications (NVQs)[19].

Post-16 students have decided to stay on at school to achieve specific educational objectives within the context of a general education. There are three main types of post-16 courses: A/AS-level courses, GNVQ and NVQ – with the possibility of combinations between them. Most sixth forms will offer both A/AS-level and one or more GNVQ or equivalent vocational courses. Courses leading to GCSE or other approved qualifications such as the International and/or the Technical Baccalaureate may also be provided.

The inspection needs to consider the quality of the whole curriculum followed by individual students. Schools must meet the general requirements of Section 1 of the 1988 Education Reform Act for post-16 students and include provision for religious education. The post-16 curriculum will normally contain additional elements such as: general studies (which may lead to a qualification); physical/recreational activities; careers education and guidance; personal, social and health education; and work experience, enterprise and community service activities.

■ Overall judgements about the extent to which curriculum provision meets the needs of all pupils should draw on the inspection of individual subjects and courses. In evaluating the curriculum for KS2 (in middle schools), KS3 and KS4, inspectors should consider evidence about all the school's provision, including provision which meets National Curriculum and religious education requirements, the provision for personal and social education and for careers education and guidance (where appropriate), and the contribution of extra-curricular activities and external links. When evaluating the post-16 curriculum inspectors should consider evidence of all the school's provision for its students.

Judgements are also required on the effectiveness of systems of assessment across the curriculum and the use of assessment for curriculum planning.

---

19 NVQs require students' competences to be assessed in the workplace or through simulated activities and for this reason relatively few schools will offer them. The full GNVQ is normally part of post-16 provision; Part One GNVQs, taken from the full GNVQ, may be offered at KS4. All courses require substantial records of students' work and internal and external verification of the standards of their work. Part One GNVQs are designed to occupy time equivalent to two GCSE subjects and to be broadly equivalent to the demands of GCSE. Pupils maintain a portfolio of work based on a vocational area and core skills in the application of number, communication and IT. At intermediate level, the core skills are deemed equivalent to GCSE grade C in English and Mathematics.

USING THE CRITERIA

Is the curriculum balanced and broadly based? Does it promote pupils' intellectual, physical and personal development and prepare pupils for the next stage of education, training, or employment?

■ Inspectors need to establish whether the curriculum complies with Section 1 of the 1988 Education Reform Act. Documentation, including the school's curriculum policy, guidelines and schemes of work, will be a starting point for consideration of whether the whole curriculum makes broad and balanced provision for all aspects of pupils' development.

For 14-16 year olds, it is essential to consider the curriculum in the light of the Dearing Review, which resulted in:

◆ enhanced flexibility for schools by reducing the mandatory curriculum to a minimum of full GCSEs in English, mathematics and science; short courses in technology and a modern foreign language; physical education; religious education and sex education;

◆ schools being enabled to exploit this additional flexibility by making available other academic options and a wider range of vocational options designed to facilitate progression to vocational courses post-16.

The curriculum at KS4 should be judged in terms of the extent to which schools meet these national intentions.

Provision at KS4 and post-16 should ensure that individual pupils and students develop their understanding of adult life and are in a position to proceed to appropriate education, training or employment options. The school's provision should include sound and impartial careers education and guidance.

It is important that inspectors examine whether post-16 students are following courses which reflect their academic or vocational aspirations and their previous achievements, and have a good chance of achieving their objectives.

Discussions with pupils and students and analysis of a sample of individual timetables may be helpful in establishing how the curriculum works in practice. Inspectors should also consider the available information on the destinations of school leavers.

Does the curriculum meet statutory requirements to teach the subjects of the National Curriculum, religious education and sex education, where these apply?

■ Provided statutory requirements are met it is for the school to determine the character of its curriculum and the mode of its delivery. Judgements about its effectiveness should be based on how well the organisation of the curriculum and its assessment contribute to pupils' attainment, progress and response rather than on pre-determined notions of what is desirable in curriculum organisation.

Guidance on using the schedule

The National Curriculum is usually taught as discrete subjects; some schools may teach parts of it in an integrated form, in a modular form or as a combination of these. Whichever approach is adopted, planning and teaching need to pay due regard to the subject Orders. Religious education may be part of or associated with a programme of personal and social education. If this is the case inspectors need to be able to identify how the requirements of the syllabus are met throughout the age range. In any case, adequate time needs to be made available for the different subjects. The test is whether pupils are able to cover the required material in appropriate depth.

The governing body of a maintained secondary school has a statutory duty to provide sex education. Parents should be consulted and informed about the policy and provision and should be informed about their rights to withdraw their children from some elements of the sex education programme. Sex education will often be found as part of a broader programme of health education. (Additional notes are given at the end of this section.)

A PRU is not required to follow a basic curriculum. However, inspectors should evaluate whether the curriculum is close enough to the National Curriculum to enable pupils to re-integrate successfully into school.

Does the curriculum provide equality of access and opportunity for pupils to learn and to make progress?

■ Inspectors should evaluate how curriculum planning and implementation take account of pupils' age, attainment, gender, ethnicity, competence in English as an additional language and special educational need, through the use of appropriate teaching methods and materials. The curriculum should respond to the cultural heritage of pupils and promote equality of opportunity. Inspectors need to consider the impact of the organisation of pupils into class and teaching groups on ensuring equality of access and opportunity.

The National Curriculum programmes of study for each key stage should be taught to all pupils. For some pupils, material may be selected from earlier or later key stages to enable them to progress and demonstrate achievement, but this material should be in contexts suitable for their ages.

Does the curriculum meet the curricular requirements of all pupils on the school's Code of Practice special education needs register?

■ Inspectors should evaluate whether the curriculum for pupils with special educational needs meets the specific needs identified in the learning objectives in individual education plans, and for pupils at stage 5, in their statements of special educational need and annual reviews.

Pupils' access to the full curriculum should not be compromised by their withdrawal for additional support for any learning difficulties. In exceptional circumstances primary schools may disapply or modify parts of the National Curriculum for individual pupils. An alternative curriculum must be provided that meets the requirements of Section 1 of the 1988 Education Reform Act.

Is the curriculum planned effectively, providing continuity and progression of learning?

■ Inspectors should evaluate whether curriculum planning takes account of what has gone before and what will follow. The need for continuity and progression applies to the whole curriculum and to individual subjects and courses; it applies between years, between key stages and between schools and colleges. Evidence is needed of whether, as pupils move between classes and key stages, the curriculum builds systematically on previous experience and existing knowledge, understanding and skills.

Inspectors should establish as far as they can the effectiveness of the school's systems for liaison with primary or middle schools and with further and higher education institutions and employers as pupils and students make the transition to further education, training or employment. Evidence is most likely to come from discussion with senior staff and teachers, and from study of a sample of pupils' records and work, but the issue may also feature in the parents' meeting.

Is the curriculum enriched by extra-curricular provision, including sport?

■ Inspectors must inspect and report on the quality, time spent and range of games offered as part of the physical education curriculum and on the provision of sport outside formal lessons, paying particular attention to traditional team games. Reports should include pupil participation rates in extra-curricular sport, the number of teachers who supervise this activity, sports competitions within and between schools and any improvement the school has made in providing both curricular and extra-curricular competitive games. Most secondary schools provide a range of extra-curricular activities, arrange visits to special events such as exhibitions and concerts, and organise sporting events, often involving other schools. PRUs may have no sports facilities.

Does the curriculum include, for pupils of secondary age, careers education and impartial guidance, drawing on the careers service?

■ Careers education should provide a planned programme to develop skills, knowledge and attitudes relating to choices and transitions to further education, training and employment. Careers guidance requires a systematic and personalised approach to helping pupils make choices appropriate to them through impartial advice. Both elements, careers education and guidance, should be part of a wider approach to preparing pupils for adult life.

The school's documentation should show how careers education is co-ordinated, how it draws on pupils' experience within subjects and is enhanced by links with employers and training providers, for example through work experience. Inspectors need to look for evidence that work experience is well-planned, effectively monitored and followed up. The effectiveness of the school's links with employers in this and other ways should be reported in Section 5.5.

In relation to careers guidance, inspectors need to judge how effectively the school provides impartial and well-informed advice, drawing on the expertise of outside agencies, particularly the careers service. The school's liaison with the careers service should be based on a clear specification of what each party will arrange and provide. By agreement with the pupil and the interviewer, inspectors may find it helpful to sit in on a few careers interviews; the key outcomes should include awareness and understanding by the pupil of the implications of choices, including knowledge of the full range of options at transition points. Inspectors need to check that the information available to pupils relating to further and higher education, training and employment is up to date, accessible, comprehensive and appropriate for the range of pupils in the school.

Inspectors need to judge whether careers education and guidance is objective and even-handed. It must also be free from gender or other stereotyping – for example, in encouraging girls as well as boys towards careers in science and engineering.

Guidance on using the schedule

Consideration should be given to whether those involved in providing careers education and guidance have access to appropriate professional development to prepare and assist them in their work. Professional development is covered in Section 6.2.

Are there effective systems for assessing pupils' attainment?

Is assessment information used to inform curriculum planning?

■ Inspectors should evaluate whether assessments are accurate and used to plan future work and to help pupils to make progress. They need to establish whether the teachers' assessments relate accurately to the National Curriculum requirements and external validation arrangements, where these apply.

A review of documentation and discussion with teachers and staff responsible for co-ordination and liaison provides a context for the assessment observed in lessons. Particular attention needs to be given to the use of assessment data in planning a response to the needs of individual pupils – for example in modifying teaching programmes for pupils with special educational needs.

In relation to National Curriculum requirements, evidence includes comparison of pupils' work with teachers' assessments and records. Teachers do not need to keep detailed records to support the assessments they make of each pupil: they need only collect samples of work which exemplify attainment at each level. Inspectors should use these samples to examine the comparability of individual teachers' judgements.

In vocational education courses in both KS4 and post-16, assessment may involve teachers working closely with people in industry, commerce or services.

Pupil records have a key role in ensuring that information on pupils' performance is transferred and used as they move through the school and from one stage of education to the next. Schools must keep formal educational records on every pupil, including material on academic achievements, other skills and abilities and progress in school, and must update these records at least once a year. Parents of pupils up to age 17 (and pupils aged 16 or over) must be given access to these records and they must be transferred if the pupil moves to another school. Assessment results may only be disclosed to another school after admission.

MAIN SOURCES OF EVIDENCE

Before the inspection

◆ the *Headteacher's Form* and the school prospectus should show, at least in outline, how far the school's planned curriculum meets statutory requirements;

◆ curriculum policies, guidelines or schemes of work will provide an indication of the extent to which the planned curriculum meets the inspection criteria;

◆ curriculum audits or analyses if available may offer useful insights;

◆ discussion at pre-inspection meetings with the headteacher, governors and parents will provide a range of perspectives on the curriculum;

◆ information supplied by the local TEC (Training and Enterprise Council) through the school may contain significant evidence about course provision, links with business, careers education and guidance, and details of locally agreed targets;

During the inspection

A comparison of curriculum plans and practice comes from:

◆ observation of lessons including shadowing individual pupils' experience of the curriculum, including extra-curricular activities for all pupils;

◆ a scrutiny of samples of pupils' work and pupils' records, including records of NC assessments;

◆ discussion with teachers, support staff and pupils concentrating on how curriculum organisation affects pupils' attainment and progress;

◆ an examination of individual education plans, statements and annual reviews will help to establish the appropriateness of provision for pupils with special educational needs.

Guidance on using the schedule

ADDITIONAL NOTES

HEALTH EDUCATION

Health education should play a major role in promoting the physical, social and mental well-being of pupils. Aspects of health education are found in subjects (for example, within the programmes of study for science) and in the daily routines of the school. Provision may also make an important contribution to pupils' personal development including moral, social and cultural aspects. Inspectors will need to establish whether provision is planned, coherent and appropriate to the ages and needs of pupils, and whether pupils have a sound knowledge and understanding of health issues and an awareness of their ability to make choices relating to their health.

Sex education and drug misuse are important elements of health education provision. School staff and other providers need to be well briefed and sensitive to the agreed approach to health education in the school and to the ages and needs of pupils.

DRUGS EDUCATION

The National Curriculum Science Order states the statutory minimum that pupils should be taught about drugs. Schools are free to decide for themselves how best to organise drug education for their pupils. They may provide it within science lessons, as appropriate within other subject areas, or as part of a broader programme of personal and social or health education. The essential aim of drug education should be to give pupils the facts, emphasise the benefits of a healthy lifestyle, and give young people the knowledge and skills to make informed and healthy choices now and later in life.

Inspectors should also determine whether schools have clear policies and procedures for dealing with drug-related incidents on the school premises and for working with other services concerned with young people to offer appropriate support and advice. DFEE Circular 4/95 offers guidance on drug education and the management of drug-related incidents.

GENERAL NATIONAL VOCATIONAL QUALIFICATIONS (GNVQS)

GNVQs are broad-based vocational qualifications which cover a wide range of occupational areas and provide opportunities to prepare pupils for further and higher education and employment. The awards are designed primarily for full-time students between the ages of 16 and 19. Part One GNVQs, taken from the full GNVQ, may be offered at KS4 and are designed to occupy time equivalent to two GCSE subjects and to be broadly equivalent to the demands of GCSE. Relatively few schools offer NVQs because of the requirement to assess competencies in the workplace or through simulated activities.

GNVQs are available at three levels: **Advanced** GNVQ, or 'vocational A-Level', is equivalent to at least two GCE A-levels, NVQ level 3 or BTEC National Certificates/Diplomas; **Intermediate** GNVQ is equivalent to four or five GCSEs at grades A to C, NVQ Level 2, or BTEC First Certificates/Diplomas; **Foundation** GNVQ is equivalent to four GCSEs graded D-G or NVQ level 1.

Each GNVQ is made up of four types of unit:

◆   mandatory vocational units covering the skills, knowledge and understanding needed for a broad range of jobs;

◆   mandatory core skills units, which further develop skills in communication, application of number and IT. The core skills units are outlined at five levels of attainment and these have been broadly linked with the National Curriculum. Students can be encouraged to work to levels of attainment in core skills units at levels above their main award;

◆   optional vocational units, which give students an opportunity to specialise;

◆   additional units, which allow for further study, for example, Personal skills – working with others; Personal skills – improving own learning and performance; Problem-solving.

Each unit is expressed in the form of elements (which describe the activity to be assessed); performance criteria (which provide a means of judging successful performance of the activity), range statements (which describe the range of settings in which the activity should be performed successfully) and evidence indicators (which describe the type and sufficiency of evidence that should be presented for assessment). These, together with the compulsory requirement for a pass in an end-of-unit test, are the means of setting the national standard. Tasks and assignments are assessed against the standards. Work assessed as a pass can be further graded according to additional criteria for the award of merit or distinction. Inspectors will need to determine whether there are appropriate systems for assessment and recording and for internal verification to check the standard of pupils' work.

The GNVQ framework enables a flexible approach to delivery. The outcomes of various activities – for example, assignments, projects, work experience, group discussion – are collected in a portfolio which is used as evidence for assessment. Because these courses are based on assessment in relation to outcomes, it is not possible to rely only on classroom observation as a means of judging standards of attainment. Inspectors will need to talk with students and scrutinise completed work in order to evaluate what pupils know, understand and can do in the vocational area and in the core skills. Inspectors will need to evaluate whether the completed work meets the GNVQ criteria and whether it is at an appropriate level of knowledge, understanding and intellectual skills, for the level of the course and its stated equivalence (GCSE or GCE A-level).

The components of the course should be well co-ordinated and provision coherent. Vocational units should be staffed by teachers who have a good knowledge and understanding of the vocational and occupational areas and the contribution of these to further stages of education, training and employment. The core skills element of courses should be appropriately designed or taught by teachers experienced in English, mathematics and IT teaching. GNVQ courses should, where appropriate, include fieldwork, visits and simulations. These elements frequently require that the school has established appropriate links with local industry, commerce and the community.

5.3 PUPILS' SPIRITUAL, MORAL, SOCIAL AND CULTURAL DEVELOPMENT

INSPECTORS MUST EVALUATE AND REPORT ON

■ the strengths and weaknesses of the school's provision for the spiritual, moral, social and cultural development of all pupils, through the curriculum and life of the school, the example set for pupils by adults in the school; and the quality of collective worship[20].

Judgements should be based on the extent to which the school:

◆ provides its pupils with knowledge and insight into values and beliefs and enables them to reflect on their experiences in a way which develops their spiritual awareness and self-knowledge;

◆ teaches the principles which distinguish right from wrong;

◆ encourages pupils to relate positively to others, take responsibility, participate fully in the community, and develop an understanding of citizenship;

◆ teaches pupils to appreciate their own cultural traditions and the diversity and richness of other cultures.

---

[20] The report should state, in Section 6.1, the school's compliance with statutory requirements, where these apply.

Guidance on using the schedule

INSPECTION FOCUS

■ Evaluation of provision for pupils' spiritual, moral, social and cultural development links four aspects of personal development in which schools have an important part to play. In this section inspectors need to evaluate what schools actively do to *promote* pupils' development. Although each aspect of spiritual, moral, social and cultural development can be viewed separately, provision is likely to be interconnected and evaluation should reflect this.

There is a strong link with sections 4.2, 5.1 and 5.2: the curriculum and its teaching provide the major vehicle for promoting personal development in all its forms. A major part is also played by the relationships that are established in a school and the support and guidance provided for pupils, covered in Section 5.4, and by the partnership with parents and the community, covered in Section 5.5.

■ In many schools the responsibility which the class tutor carries can facilitate a coherent approach to pupils' spiritual, moral, social and cultural development and its connections with intellectual development. The approach should be informed by links with parents and enriched by contact with the community the school serves.

Inspectors should evaluate the extent to which provision reaches all pupils whatever their background. Pupils with special educational needs may need additional support and encouragement to take a full part in school activities and to accept and exercise responsibilities.

■ Overall judgements are concerned with the opportunities given for pupils to learn about and explore different values, beliefs and views and to develop and express their own. Judgements should be based on evidence from the whole curriculum and the day-to-day life of the school, including the examples set by adults and the quality of collective worship. This is an area on which evidence must be drawn from all members of the team before considered corporate judgements are made. The judgements are best made in conjunction with those on other aspects of provision.

USING THE CRITERIA

Does the school provide its pupils with knowledge and insight into values and religious beliefs and enable them to reflect on their experiences in a way which develops their self-knowledge and spiritual awareness?

■ Effective provision for spiritual development depends on a curriculum and approaches to teaching which embody clear values and provide opportunities for pupils to gain understanding by developing a sense of curiosity through reflection on their own and other people's lives and beliefs, their environment and the human condition. It relies on teachers receiving and valuing pupils' ideas across the whole curriculum, for example, in literature, art, music, history and religious education. Acts of collective worship play a particular part. To the extent that spiritual insights imply an awareness of how pupils relate to others, there is a strong link to both moral and social development.

Guidance on using the schedule

Although religious education and spiritual development are not synonymous, religious education can make a significant contribution to spiritual development. Inspectors might consider, for example, whether pupils are encouraged to: consider life's fundamental questions and how religious teaching can relate to them; respond to such questions with reference to the teachings and practices of religions as well as from their own experience and viewpoint; and reflect on their own beliefs or values in the light of what they are studying in religious education.

Inspection of acts of collective worship is needed in all schools which do not provide denominational education. Evaluation should focus on whether acts of worship are well planned and encourage pupils to explore questions about meaning and purpose, values and beliefs. Compliance with statutory requirements on collective worship should be reported in Section 6.1. (Guidance on the inspection of collective worship is given at the end of this section.)

Does the school teach the principles which separate right from wrong?

■ The essence of moral development is to build a framework of values which regulate personal behaviour through principles rather than through fear of punishment or reward. Pupils are able to make moral decisions through the application of reason, even though they may not cope quite so securely with problems in which they are emotionally involved: in other words, their learning about moral issues may be on a different plane from their behaviour. Moral and social education are closely related and depend on the school fostering values such as honesty, fairness and respect for truth and justice.

Inspectors should consider whether the school provides a moral code as a basis for behaviour which is promoted through the life of the school. They should also look at the opportunities for pupils to develop and express moral values and extend social and personal understanding across a range of issues, including, for example, personal rights and responsibilities and equal opportunities. In all areas of the curriculum pupils can be encouraged to explore ideas about such issues. The moral and social issues raised through the study of warfare, the interaction of people, resources and the environment, and the ways in which science and technology can affect our lives, are further examples. Sensitive discussion of incidents that arise in school or outside it may be used to help pupils distinguish right from wrong behaviour.

Does the school encourage pupils to relate effectively to others, take responsibility, participate fully in the community and develop an understanding of citizenship?

■ Social development hinges on an acceptance of group rules and the ability to set oneself in a wider context. Adolescents may find that the need to be socially compliant is sometimes at odds with their developing moral sensibility. Partly for this reason, the quality of relationships in schools is of crucial importance in forming pupils' attitudes to good social behaviour and self-discipline.

Inspectors need to consider how the school, through its organisation, curriculum and other activities, contributes to social development through experience and understanding of social relationships and the rights and responsibilities of individuals within the social setting. Evidence may include opportunities for pupils to work co-operatively in lessons, on projects or in games involving competition, discipline and fair play. Account should be taken of opportunities for pupils to take on responsibility, demonstrate initiative and contribute to the life of the school as a community. Vocational courses at KS4 and post-16 can play a significant part in this development.

Does the school teach pupils to appreciate and develop their own cultural traditions and appreciate the diversity and richness of other cultures?

■ Cultural development is concerned with both participation in and appreciation of cultural traditions.

The school's approach should be active. Inspectors need to look for evidence of how the school seeks to enrich its pupils' knowledge and experience of their own and other cultural traditions, through the curriculum and through visits, clubs and other activities. Aspects of the curriculum such as history, geography, art, music, dance, drama, literature and the study of language can all contribute positively, for example, through opportunities for pupils to:

◆ visit museums and art galleries;

◆ work with artists, authors and performers;

◆ develop openness towards and value the music and dance of different cultures;

◆ appreciate the natural world through art and literature;

◆ recognise the contribution of many cultures to mathematics and to scientific and technological development.

Guidance on using the schedule

MAIN SOURCES OF EVIDENCE

Before the inspection

◆ **analysis of the school's aims and other documentation,** including curriculum guidance, gives a preliminary view of how the school seeks to promote pupils' spiritual, moral, social and cultural development;

◆ **discussion with the headteacher, governors and parents** at pre-inspection meetings, and the returns from the questionnaire provide a range of perspectives on provision and the values promoted by the school.

During the inspection

Evidence of the quality, range and impact of provision can be found through:

◆ **observation of lessons and the daily routines** in and around the school; collective worship and assemblies; extra-curricular activities;

◆ **scrutiny of syllabi** (particularly the agreed syllabus for RE), curriculum guidelines and schemes of work including, if applicable, personal and social education programmes;

◆ **examination of the range and quality of resources** used to bring pupils into contact with different aspects of social and cultural traditions;

◆ **observation of pupils' responsibilities** around the school and opportunities for pupils' own initiatives;

◆ **discussion with pupils, teachers and other adults** on the moral values of the school; whether pupils are treated in accordance with these values and whether pupils' contributions are valued by adults.

◆ **observation to establish whether pupils are treated consistently.**

Guidance on using the schedule

ADDITIONAL NOTES

COLLECTIVE WORSHIP

The law requires schools other than PRUs to provide a daily act of collective worship. Taken over a term, the majority of such acts of worship should be wholly or mainly of a broadly Christian character. The school prospectus should make clear parents' right to withdraw their children from collective worship. Defining worship is difficult because a wide variety of activities is used by people of all faiths. In forming a judgement about the character and quality of worship in schools, the following points may be helpful:

◆ worship is generally understood to imply the recognition of a supreme being. It should be clear that the words used and/or the activities observed in worship recognise the existence of a deity;

◆ much that is identifiably Christian in tone, may not necessarily mention Jesus. This is true of some hymns and prayers used regularly as part of worship within Christian churches. However, if the worship consistently avoids reference to Jesus within the spoken or written word then it could not reasonably be defined as mainly Christian;

◆ collective worship should not be judged by the presence or absence of a particular ingredient. It might include: sharing values of a Christian nature; opportunities for prayers or meditation; opportunities to reflect upon readings from holy texts or other writings which bring out religious themes; performance of music, drama and/or dance;

◆ each act of worship in a school should be considered as a piece. Before reaching a judgement the activities observed during the inspection should be set alongside the evidence of what has occurred, and is planned, over a term. If on balance it is judged that what the school provides is not in keeping with the spirit of the law, then this should be recorded and the reason(s) given. (Section 6.1 covers non-compliance with statutory requirements.);

◆ worship may be judged not to fulfil statutory requirements but could still be observed to make a powerful contribution to spiritual, moral, social and cultural development. That should be made clear in the report.

Inspection schedule

5.4 SUPPORT, GUIDANCE AND PUPILS' WELFARE[21]

INSPECTORS MUST EVALUATE AND REPORT ON

- strengths and weaknesses in the school's provision for the educational and personal support and guidance of pupils and its contribution to educational standards achieved, taking account of individual needs, and the steps taken to ensure pupils' welfare;

- the school's arrangements for child protection;

- any matters which, in the view of inspectors, constitute a threat to health and safety.

Judgements should be based on the extent to which the school:

- provides effective support and advice for all its pupils, informed by monitoring of their academic progress, personal development, behaviour and attendance;

- has effective measures to promote discipline and good behaviour and eliminate oppressive behaviour including all forms of harassment and bullying;

- has effective child protection procedures;

- is successful in promoting the health, safety and general well-being of its pupils.

---

[21] Where boarding provision is included in the contract, evaluation of its quality should be included in this section of the report.

Guidance on using the schedule

INSPECTION FOCUS

■ The school's support and guidance should enable all pupils to take full advantage of the educational opportunities offered and have high but realistic expectations of themselves. The inspection judgements should focus on the extent to which these ends are achieved through effective monitoring of personal and educational progress, through individual support and advice, and through a climate in which pupils' well-being is paramount.

■ Effective support and guidance is based on the informal relationships which pervade the school, the planned curriculum and the consistent implementation of clear policies. Day-to-day support and guidance are normally provided by the class tutor with contributions from other staff. The class tutor may be responsible for monitoring pupils' academic progress as well as their personal development. Guidance in relation to personal and social education may take place through specific programmes within the curriculum.

Pupils with special educational needs are usually supported within the general class group, but in some schools support may be within a special base. Some pupils may require regular medical supervision and/or therapy. Individual education plans for some pupils may include objectives related to attitudes to learning and behaviour. Pupils with emotional and behavioural difficulties may need additional pastoral support.

Essential to the effectiveness of any school are the arrangements for promoting regular attendance, good behaviour and respect for others. Action to prevent and deal with harassment and bullying are normally part of the school's behaviour and discipline policy and may feature in teaching programmes.

Schools will normally have regular contacts with other agencies such as the careers service, the health, police, psychological and social services, and these agencies will contribute to the support and guidance of pupils. In relation to child protection, schools have responsibility for reporting to, and liaising with, other agencies on the progress of children placed on the child protection register.

■ Overall judgements about support, guidance and welfare need to draw on the evidence of the whole team from all aspects of the school's work.

Any matters which in the view of the inspectors constitute a serious threat to the health and safety of staff and visitors as well as pupils must be reported in this section and in the key issues for action. Where there is a breach of statutory requirements, this should be reported in Section 6.1.

Guidance on using the schedule

USING THE CRITERIA

Does the school provide effective support, advice and guidance for all its pupils, informed by monitoring of their academic progress, personal development, behaviour and attendance?

■ Inspectors should assess how well staff interact with pupils within and outside the classroom, their accessibility and responsiveness to pupils' needs and the quality of the support they give. The key is the impact on pupils' progress, general confidence and ability to cope effectively with everyday life in the school. In relation to pupils with special educational needs, particular attention should be paid to how pupils are helped to meet the objectives in their individual education plans. Inspectors need to assess the quality of liaison with support agencies and the impact on support for pupils. Where inspection priorities allow, it may be possible to discuss this with visiting staff.

In relation to attendance, inspectors should establish whether the requirements for recording and reporting attendance are met, how the school follows up any unauthorised absence and any ways in which it monitors and seeks to improve attendance, in conjunction, for example, with the LEA. They should also consider, where appropriate, the support given to pupils who have had a prolonged period of absence.

Does the school have effective measures to promote discipline and good behaviour and eliminate oppressive behaviour including all forms of harassment and bullying?

■ While evidence of the school's intentions can be gained from documents on policy and procedures, the emphasis should be on the consistency of practice. Evaluation against the criterion should link with Section 4.2. Attention should be given to how the school raises general awareness of behaviour issues and how it creates a climate for good behaviour, as well as how it deals with specific incidents of misbehaviour. During the inspection, observation, discussion with staff and with pupils and analysis of records will provide the basis for judgements.

In relation to harassment and bullying, inspectors need to assess how well the school recognises and records incidents that occur, how well it deals with them and what steps are taken to prevent repetition.

Does the school have effective child protection procedures?

■ Inspectors should evaluate whether the school is in a position to comply with local child protection procedures and whether the school's approach helps pupils to protect themselves and understand the importance of protecting others. A particular focus is how the school deals with instances of possible child abuse and its procedures for liaison with other agencies where children are on the child protection register. Inspectors should establish whether all staff are aware of the procedures and how they raise pupils' awareness of child protection issues.

Where the registered inspector has reasonable grounds to believe that specific instances of possible child abuse are not being dealt with satisfactorily by the school, the relevant authority, normally the social services child protection team, should be contacted.

Additional notes on child protection are given at the end of this section.

Is the school successful in promoting the health, safety and general well-being of its pupils?

■ Inspectors should judge whether the school does all it reasonably can to protect the pupils in its charge from harm, and promotes their well-being through awareness of health and safety and through its day-to-day procedures. Evidence will come from examination of documents, from discussions and from observations of procedures such as those covering the organisation of school meals, the care of property and the arrangements for and the conduct of visits. Attention should be given to the first-aid and other medical support given by the school, including arrangements for pupils with specific physical or medical needs. Inspectors should be alert to features of the premises, equipment or working practices of the school which may impact on pupils' well-being.

Additional notes on health and safety are given at the end of this section.

MAIN SOURCES OF EVIDENCE

Before the inspection

◆ **the meeting with parents** provides important evidence on the provision and effectiveness of pupils' support and guidance;

◆ **the pre-inspection visit** will give an indication of whether there is a suitable climate for the support, guidance and welfare of pupils;

◆ further evidence will derive from the **prospectus, staff handbook (if available) and other available policy documents.**

During the inspection

◆ **observation and discussion with pupils** will establish whether policy and practice correspond and if there is consistency across the school;

◆ **discussion with staff** will provide useful insight into procedures for dealing with harassment, bullying and child protection, and whether these are understood and consistently applied;

◆ **observation** of informal support given to pupils;

◆ **discussion** with the education welfare officer and visiting staff from the agencies where practicable;

◆ **health and safety issues,** in relation to the accommodation and site, school routines and practices, and visits.

ADDITIONAL NOTES

CHILD PROTECTION

Schools play an important part in protecting children and a high percentage of children at risk are referred by teachers. All schools need to be vigilant because incidence of sexual and emotional abuse is not related to social and economic circumstances.

DFE Circular 4/88 gave guidance on child protection procedures within the education service. This circular was part of an inter-agency approach which was subsequently strengthened and revised by the Children Act 1989. Further inter-agency guidance can be found in *Working Together under the Children Act 1989: a guide to arrangements for inter-agency co-operation for the protection of children from abuse*. Inspectors should establish that schools comply with this guidance by:

◆ designating a senior member of staff to have responsibility under procedures established by the Area Child Protection Committee (ACPC) and the LEA for co-ordinating action within the school and liaison with other agencies;

◆ following local ACPC procedures and promptly referring suspected cases of child abuse to the local social services department, or to the police, which are the investigative agencies in case of child protection;

◆ liaising with all other agencies involved in the protection of children, by monitoring the progress of children placed on the child protection register, by submitting reports to social services departments and case conferences, and by being represented at child protection case conferences;

◆ contributing to the prevention of child abuse through teaching which builds awareness of the dangers of abuse, helps children to protect themselves and develops responsible attitudes to adult life and parenthood;

◆ taking part in training which leads to a greater understanding of the signs and symptoms of child abuse, familiarises participants with ACPC and LEA procedures for dealing with individual cases, informs them about the roles and responsibilities of the other agencies with whom the school has to liaise, and gives advice on making use of the curriculum to build preventive approaches to child protection.

HEALTH AND SAFETY

Controlling health and safety risks is an essential part of educational provision. The emphasis in the inspection should be on the extent to which the school responds to statutory requirements to establish, monitor and review the effectiveness of safe working procedures. Inspectors are not expected to carry out an audit of health and safety practice but to report on what they see.

The registered inspector will need to:

◆ check that the school is aware of the need to comply with statutory requirements for health and safety and has clear procedures to identify and control health and safety risks;

◆ judge whether the school has a responsible attitude towards the education and training of pupils in safety procedures;

◆ record any health and safety irregularities observed during the inspection and bring these to the attention of the headteacher and, where potentially serious, the employer;

◆ alert the Health and Safety Executive where there is an imminent risk of serious injury and the employer appears likely to refuse to remedy the situation as a matter or urgency;

◆ record serious matters in the inspection report, in the key issues for action.

Before the inspection the registered inspector should establish through the *Headteacher's Statement* that the school has a policy and procedures to identify, control, record and report health and safety risks. Important features are:

◆ a written statement of health and safety policy;

◆ the designation of one or more members of staff responsible for the implementation of policy;

◆ procedures for monitoring and reporting;

◆ arrangements for dealing with accidents and emergencies;

◆ details of health and safety training of staff with particular responsibilities, such as first aid, the use of specified materials and equipment, the supervision of outdoor activities;

◆ a record of any identified health and safety concerns and the action taken or proposed.

During the inspection inspectors should judge the extent to which the policy and procedures are known and put into practice. Inspectors will need to take account of health and safety when evaluating pupils' behaviour, the accommodation and site, the learning resources, the teaching and the provision of educational activities, including visits. They should, for example, be alert to evidence of:

◆ safe practice in play areas, classrooms and specialist areas;

◆ attention to health and safety in the preparation and conduct of visits out of school;

◆ pupils' knowledge of safe working procedures;

◆ provision of a safe environment with due attention to the layout, placement of equipment and materials, the condition of floors and play areas;

◆ equipment which is well maintained and in safe condition;

◆ general cleanliness of floors and surfaces;

◆ appropriate arrangements for the provision, storage, administration and recording of first aid equipment and medication;

◆ clean and suitable arrangements for the consumption of food.

Guidance on using the schedule

Subject inspectors will need to establish that safe procedures are followed in their respective fields[22]. These include, for example, whether pupils are using eye or face shields in science and technology during practical work; whether machines and equipment are in safe positions in workshops; whether kilns are guarded to prevent pupils from touching hot surfaces; and whether flammable and corrosive substances are correctly stored.

---

22   For guidance on health and safety issues in subjects of the curriculum, useful references are:
Safety in Science Education, DFEE, 1995; *Managing Health and Safety in School Workshops*, National Association of Advisers and Inspectors of Design and Technology (NAAIDT); *Managing Health and Safety in Food and Textiles*, National Association of Advisors and Inspectors of Design and Technology (NAAIDT); *Health and Safety in Workshops* BS4163; *Safe Practice in Physical Education*, British Association of Advisers and Lecturers in PE (BAALPE).

Inspection schedule

5.5 PARTNERSHIP WITH PARENTS AND THE COMMUNITY

INSPECTORS MUST EVALUATE AND REPORT ON

■ the effectiveness of the school's partnership with parents, highlighting strengths and weaknesses, in terms of:

i the information provided about the school and about pupils' work and progress through annual and other reports and parents' meetings;

ii parents' involvement with the work of the school and with their children's work at home;

■ the contribution which the school's links with the community make to pupils' attainment and personal development.

Judgements should be based on the extent to which:

◆ links with parents contribute to pupils' learning;

◆ the school's work is enriched by links with the community, including employers, and provision for work experience for pupils of secondary age;

◆ the school promotes pupils' contributions to the local community, including through voluntary service in secondary schools.

INSPECTION FOCUS

■ The focus of inspection should be on the extent to which parents support the work of the school and are informed about their children's progress. Similarly, inspectors should look at the way in which the school involves the local community and how this affects pupils' attainment, progress and personal development.

■ In secondary schools, contact between school and home is often the responsibility of the class tutor or head of year, although the nature of the contact and the extent to which parents are involved in knowing what their children are doing, how they are getting on and how to help them will be a matter of school policy. Many schools actively promote the partnership with parents through, for example, induction programmes, regular meetings and activities, enlisting their help with visits and involving parents in pupils' work.

The arrangements for reporting to parents vary but are based on the statutory requirements to give regular information about pupils' attainment and opportunities for parents to discuss progress. Pupils with special educational needs who have individual education plans will have regular reviews and those with statements must have an annual review, involving parents as well as support agencies.

Many schools have close links with the local community, Training and Enterprise Councils (TECs), and local industry, commerce and services. Some are used directly to enrich the curriculum provision; others, such as involvement with charities and local organisations, contribute to pupils' personal development.

■ Overall judgements need to establish whether:

  ◆ there are clear lines of communication;

  ◆ the school's approach to relations with parents is maintained consistently;

  ◆ the school does all it can to gain the involvement of all parents.

In relation to links with the community, judgements need to draw on the range of activities and their effect on pupils' attainment, progress and personal development.

USING THE CRITERIA

Do links with parents contribute to pupils' learning?

■ Evaluation should focus on the extent to which the school involves parents as partners in their children's learning. Evidence of parental involvement will derive from discussion and observation and from assessing the quality of information provided for parents, including the prospectus. Inspectors should evaluate how the school communicates information to parents for whom English is an additional language.

Guidance on using the schedule

Inspectors should explore how well the school helps parents to understand its curriculum and the teaching it provides, and to take a full part in the decisions affecting pupils' choice of subject or course.

A check should be made on how parents are kept informed about their child's progress, including whether written reports to parents meet the statutory requirements and give clear information about pupils' attainment and progress. Opportunities for follow-up should be explored. Evidence will arise from the parents' meeting, sampling of reports and discussions with staff. The school may have examples of records of regular home-school contacts, such as homework diaries. In looking at the work of a sample of pupils it can be helpful to look at copies of reports and discuss pupils' subsequent progress with teachers.

For pupils with special educational needs, inspectors should establish whether parents are involved in the formal reviews of their children's progress.

Is the school's work enriched by links with the community, including employers, and provision for work experience for pupils of secondary age?

Does the school promote pupils' contributions to the local community, including through voluntary service?

■ Evaluation should centre on the contribution made to pupils' intellectual and personal development by the school's involvement with, and contribution to, the community. There may be links with a range of organisations, services and employers, through which pupils gain, for example, a greater understanding of society and the nature of citizenship. Some links may enhance particular aspects of curriculum provision by setting teaching in a work-related context.

Where **community education** is part of the school's provision and inspected as such, inspectors will need to determine how far it serves both the school and its community, bringing local experience into the school's curriculum and extra-curricular activities, and using the school as a resource for formal and informal learning and development of the whole community.

Inspectors need to consider how the purposes of community education link with the aims of the school; whether the direction and leadership of it is clear and supportive; the range of provision made; how far provision is based on a systematic assessment of needs; how well participants achieve educational and personal goals; and how well the impact of provision on both the school and the community is monitored and evaluated. Evidence will include observation of activities in and out of school; scrutiny of plans and records, including surveys and other assessments of need; and discussions with pupils, staff and users.

MAIN SOURCES OF EVIDENCE

Before the inspection

◆ **the pre-inspection parents' meeting and completed questionnaire** should provide substantial evidence about parental understanding of, and involvement with, the work of the school;

◆ **the prospectus** and general information for parents, including newsletters and bulletins, provide further insight into the school's approach to its partnership with parents;

◆ the extent of contacts with the local community, TECs and employers are usually included in the **minutes of governors' meetings.**

During the Inspection

◆ **discussion with parents** helping with aspects of school work may provide evidence of the kinds of contact they have with the school;

◆ inspectors should read the **annual report to parents**;

◆ **discussion with pupils and scrutiny** of their work will reveal the nature of work taken home and the extent to which it involves parents;

◆ insights into partnership with the community may come from **contact with employers** about education-business links, including work-experience placements, and from information on the school's contributions to the local community.

Inspection schedule

6 The management and efficiency of the school

6.1 LEADERSHIP AND MANAGEMENT

INSPECTORS MUST EVALUATE AND REPORT ON

■ how well the governors, headteacher and staff with management responsibilities contribute to the quality of education provided by the school and standards achieved by all of its pupils;

■ the extent to which the school complies with statutory requirements.

Judgements should be based on the extent to which:

◆ strong leadership provides clear educational direction for its work;

◆ teaching and curriculum development are monitored and supported;

◆ the school has aims, values and policies which are reflected through all its work;

◆ the school, through its development planning, identifies relevant priorities and targets, takes the necessary action, and monitors and evaluates its progress towards them;

◆ there is a positive ethos, which reflects the school's commitment to high achievement, an effective learning environment, good relationships and equality of opportunity for all pupils;

◆ statutory requirements are met.

Guidance on using the schedule

INSPECTION FOCUS

■ Evaluation should focus on the extent to which leadership and management produce an effective school: one that promotes and sustains improvement in educational standards achieved and the quality of education provided.

There are three key points about the evaluation:

◆ first, the focus is on impact not intentions, although it is very important for inspectors to understand what the intentions are in order to assess how effectively they are being met;

◆ second, the judgement is about the quality and not the particular style or pattern of leadership and management. Different styles and patterns can be equally effective;

◆ third, leadership and management should be judged as a whole, taking into account the contributions of the governing body and staff, as well as the headteacher. While the personal contribution of the headteacher is crucial, the focus of inspection should not be exclusively on what the headteacher does.

■ The way in which the roles of the governing body, headteacher and staff (including support staff) are carried out may vary significantly in relation to school size and other factors. Definitions of the roles of governors, the headteacher and teaching staff are set out in education law; the issue for inspectors is how these roles are interpreted in the context of the particular school. Some PRUs may also have an advisory committee of LEA representatives, schools and the community.

The governing body has specific statutory responsibilities. These are highlighted in each section of this guidance. In essence, the governing body has three main tasks: to provide a strategic view of where the school is heading; to act as a critical friend to the school; and to hold the school to account for the educational standards it achieves and the quality of education it provides.

The headteacher is the professional leader of the school, responsible for the direction of its work and for its day-to-day management and organisation. In an effective school the headteacher, acting with senior staff, has a direct concern for the sustained improvement of quality and standards, for equality of opportunity of all pupils and for the development of policies and use of resources to achieve these ends. The headteacher or teacher in charge of a PRU may manage a wider service or the PRU may have several sites.

Other staff in the school have leadership and management roles, for example as heads of department and heads of year. Most teachers and some administrative staff hold responsibility for aspects of the school's curriculum and organisation and some hold more than one. In small schools responsibilities are often carried out informally. In a well-managed school, responsibilities are clearly defined and there is effective delegation. Staff, including support staff, understand the role they are encouraged to play in the development and running of the school.

■ Overall judgements need to be based on a wide range of evidence. They must put the emphasis on the impact of leadership and management on the work of the school, particularly in relation to its core purposes of teaching and learning. Inspectors should consider leadership and management both as a whole and in terms of co-ordination of subjects or areas of learning and responsibility for other aspects of school life. Inspectors should come to a clear view about the contribution which

Guidance on using the schedule

leadership and management make to the school's achievements, supported by evidence of, for example, whether the school:

◆ has a sense of purpose evident in all its work and in the involvement of all its staff;

◆ appreciates its strengths and how to sustain them;

◆ knows its weaknesses, at school and classroom level, and how to overcome them;

◆ establishes its priorities and sets targets for improvement, pursues its goals and reviews its progress;

◆ insists that all pupils do their best and are able to play a full part in the life of the school.

In reporting the school's compliance with statutory requirements, inspectors should focus on those which are required of the appropriate authority, especially governors. Significant matters need to be included in the **key issues for action** section of the report.

USING THE CRITERIA

Does strong leadership provide clear educational direction for the work of the school?

■ This criterion is not about an educational vision in the abstract but about a sense of purpose demonstrated in the work of the school.

Inspectors need to establish whether the governing body has developed a strategic view of the school's development and the extent to which the headteacher and senior management team provide positive leadership which gives a firm steer to the school's work. The same perspective should apply to the way heads of department and other managers carry out their responsibilities. Leadership is concerned with building and co-ordinating a team whose members have a common purpose, a willingness to contribute individual strengths to the common purpose and a capacity to reflect critically on what they are doing and how it can be improved.

Inspectors need evidence, first, of the extent to which governors' contributions in support of the headteacher and staff are informed by an understanding of their roles and of the school; and, second, of whether the proceedings of the governing body enable it to fulfil its responsibilities for strategic planning and the quality of education. Governing body papers and discussions with governors and the headteacher may illustrate particular decisions and the background to them. Identification of examples before the inspection may allow for the impact of decisions to be traced through the school's work.

Evaluation of the role of the headteacher needs to focus on the extent to which his or her professional leadership and management are effective in those aspects of the school's work which bear most directly on the improvement of the quality of provision and the educational standards achieved. Inspectors should look for evidence of the headteacher's commitment and contribution to these areas through, for example, the management of staff and pupils, the monitoring and evaluation of classroom work and through links with parents.

Evaluation of the contribution made by staff with management roles can start with whether job descriptions are clear and realistic and whether staff understand and are committed to them. Evaluation should also cover whether staff manage their responsibilities effectively in relation to the time and opportunities made available. A useful line of enquiry is the link between job descriptions, staff appraisal, staff development and the school's decision-making structure. The focus should be on what staff with management responsibilities do to establish and improve standards and quality.

Are teaching and curriculum development monitored, evaluated and supported?

■ This criterion applies to all staff with management responsibility. It emphasises that a test of effective leadership and management is the commitment to monitoring and evaluating teaching and the curriculum and to taking action to sustain and improve their quality.

Inspectors should assess how well this commitment is seen through at all levels. They should establish what the headteacher and other staff do to find out about the quality of provision and what they do to support and encourage colleagues, to build on good work and remedy weaknesses. Evaluating teaching and the curriculum should lead to specific intervention, for example through a change in curriculum organisation, through curriculum development, staff training, the provision of resources or intensive support for individual teachers. In some cases the action taken will necessarily be indirect.

The team needs to collect evidence through subject inspection about the effect of what is done to improve provision. The evidence will be pupils' attainment, progress and response. Examples of specific action may be drawn from:

◆ the school development plan and subject elements of it;

◆ the steps taken through the appraisal process and the staff development programme (covered in Section 6.2) to improve teaching;

◆ the outcomes of the monitoring of pupils' work and experience in school.

Does the school have aims, values and policies which are reflected through all its work?

■ The analysis starts with whether the school has agreed and published aims which express high expectations of what pupils can achieve.

The central question is the extent to which aims, values and policies influence the work of all staff and form the basis of a shared sense of purpose. Inspectors should establish, first, how staff are involved in the formulation of aims, values and policies and of the procedures which arise from them; and, second, what steps are taken to ensure that teaching and other staff (including staff new to the school) understand them. The test is whether they are reflected in the work of the school and kept under review.

Parents' support for the school's aims and values is reflected in the parents' questionnaire and meeting. The school may have carried out surveys of the views of parents for itself, the outcomes of which may provide valuable background information.

Inspectors should also seek evidence of the extent to which pupils feel they belong to and support the school community.

Guidance on using the schedule

Does the school, through its development planning, identify appropriate priorities and targets, take the necessary action and monitor and evaluate its progress towards them?

■ Evaluation should start with the school's planning, whether in the form of a written school development plan or otherwise. There are three elements on which evaluation needs to focus:

◆ whether the school's priorities and any specific targets associated with them are appropriate – that is, whether they are the right issues to be pursuing in relation to the school's circumstances and needs;

◆ whether the school has been able to devise clear programmes of action and target resources, particularly staff time and funding, for curriculum and staff development, and to manage the implementation within the time intended;

◆ whether the school has sound procedures for monitoring and evaluating the outcomes of its work, including the use of quantitative data where appropriate, in order to judge the extent to which priorities are achieved.

School development planning is likely to be a useful process if it involves all staff productively in these elements of planning, implementation and review. Inspectors should decide whether, taken together, they form the basis of an effective strategy for improvement.

Is there a positive ethos which reflects the school's commitment to high achievement, an effective learning environment, good relationships and equality of opportunity for all pupils?

■ Inspectors should make a summary judgement about the ethos of the school, drawing on conclusions reached in relation to other sections of the Schedule, notably Section 4.2. The focus is the contribution of leadership and management to attitudes, relationships and the provision of equal opportunities. (Notes on the management of equal opportunities and of provision for special educational needs are given at the end of this section.)

Are statutory requirements met?

■ Reference should be made to the extent to which the governing body fulfils its statutory obligations.

MAIN SOURCES OF EVIDENCE

Before the inspection

◆ the *Headteacher's Form*, school prospectus and school development plan, and policy documents should indicate the main aims and priorities of the school;

◆ a staff handbook (if available) may outline some of the main policies and procedures associated with the management of the school;

◆ job descriptions (if available) will give an initial picture of how responsibilities are set out within the school;

◆ minutes of the governing body meetings may help in forming a preliminary view of the governors' involvement in the strategic management of the school;

◆ pre-inspection discussions with headteachers, governors and parents should give an indication of how well the school's aims and priorities are understood and supported.

During the inspection

Evidence of the extent to which aims, policies and priorities are reflected in the work of the school may be gained from:

◆ observation of lessons and the daily routines of the school to establish the impact on standards achieved by pupils, and, in particular, the effectiveness of equal opportunities and special educational needs policies;

◆ discussion with staff holding significant responsibilities in the school (including heads of department and co-ordinators), establishing their role in monitoring, evaluating and intervening in the subject or aspect of work for which they have responsibility;

◆ discussion with support staff to gain their perceptions of, and support for, the aims and values of the school;

◆ discussion with pupils to gain a sense of whether the values of the school community are clear to them.

Guidance on using the schedule

ADDITIONAL NOTES

EQUAL OPPORTUNITIES

References to equal opportunities are made throughout the schedule and guidance. This section focuses upon the effectiveness of the school's leadership and management in overseeing the creation and implementation of policies to promote equality of opportunity and high achievements for all pupils.

Inspectors will need to evaluate:

◆ how far the school complies with relevant legislation, including the Education Act (1944), the Sex Discrimination Act (1975), the Race Relations Act (1976), the Education Act (1981), the Education Act (1986), the Children Act (1989), the Education Reform Act (1988) and subsequent case law;

◆ how well the leadership and management promote equal access by all pupils to the full range of opportunities for achievement that the school provides.

During the inspection the team should consider how well the school:

◆ reflects equality of opportunity in its aims and objectives, curriculum and organisation, including the grouping of pupils;

◆ monitors pupils' achievements and destinations by gender, attainment, background and ethnicity to ensure fairness of treatment;

◆ offers relevant role models to all pupils in its distribution of teachers and others within its staffing and management structures, including the allocation of curricular and other responsibilities;

◆ provides appropriate support for pupils for whom English is an additional language in order to give them access to the whole curriculum.

Evidence will need to include a scrutiny of the school's policies, staffing structures, curricular plans and pupils' records; discussions with the headteacher, other staff and pupils; direct observation of actions and relationships in and out of classrooms; consideration of the educational standards achieved by pupils, including examination and other test results; and consideration of the quality of provision under other sections of the schedule.

SPECIAL EDUCATIONAL NEEDS

References to special educational needs are made throughout the schedule and guidance. This section focuses on the fulfilment of statutory responsibilities, and on the quality and effectiveness of the general oversight and day-to-day management arrangements shared by the governing body, headteacher and other staff.

Inspectors will need to check that the school has regard to the 1994 Code of Practice on the identification and assessment of special educational need and to the earlier relevant sections of the 1993, 1988 and 1981 Education Acts. Discussions with the headteacher and governors, together with a scrutiny of the school's policies and plans, will show whether the school complies with the following requirements:

◆ that in co-operation with the headteacher, the governing body must determine the school's policy and approach for special educational needs, set up appropriate staffing and funding arrangements and maintain general oversight of special educational needs provision;

◆ that the governing body must designate either the headteacher or, in schools other than nursery schools, an appropriate governor as a 'responsible person' to oversee special educational needs in the school (the governing body may also appoint a committee to monitor overall special educational needs policy and provision);

◆ that the governing body's annual report informs parents about the success of the special educational needs policy and any significant changes to it; any consultation with the LEA, funding authority or other schools; and the allocation of resources over the previous year to pupils with special educational needs.

Inspectors will also need to determine how far the school's allocation of responsibilities and the way they are carried out are effective in promoting good and efficient use of special educational needs provision to support pupils' attainment and progress. Statutorily, the headteacher retains responsibility for all aspects of special educational needs provision but may delegate day-to-day management to a member of the senior management team or to a co-ordinator who will work with other staff and parents, drawing together policy, provision and advice to others.

Discussion with the co-ordinator, other staff, parents (if possible) and visiting specialists such as educational psychologists, should help determine how far:

◆ provision for special educational needs permeates the school's organisational and curricular structures and the practice in the school;

◆ all staff work closely with the special educational needs co-ordinator;

◆ parents know who is their main point of contact (normally the special educational needs co-ordinator) and who is the school's 'responsible person';

◆ resources, including staffing, are managed effectively and efficiently to support special educational needs policies and pupils' identified needs;

◆ all staff are sufficiently aware of procedures for identifying, assessing and providing for pupils with special educational needs;

◆ pupils' progress is monitored, especially in relation to annual reviews and individual education plans;

◆ assessment, recording and reporting satisfy statutory requirements;

◆ the use of specialist support from outside agencies is well managed within the school.

Inspection schedule

6.2 STAFFING, ACCOMMODATION AND LEARNING RESOURCES

INSPECTORS MUST EVALUATE AND REPORT ON

■ the adequacy of staffing, accommodation and learning resources, highlighting strengths and weaknesses in different subjects and areas of the curriculum, where they affect the quality of education provided and the educational standards achieved.

Judgements should be based on the extent to which:

◆ the number, qualifications and experience of teachers and other classroom staff match the demands of the curriculum;

◆ arrangements for the induction, appraisal and professional development of staff contribute to their effectiveness;

◆ the accommodation allows the curriculum to be taught effectively;

◆ learning resources are adequate for the school's curriculum and range of pupils.

Guidance on using the schedule

INSPECTION FOCUS

- The report needs to evaluate the extent to which the school is staffed and resourced to teach the curriculum effectively, and whether there are any clear features which contribute to or detract from quality and standards. Judgements on the effective use of staff, accommodation and learning resources should be included in Section 6.3.

- **Staffing** accounts for a high proportion of the school budget. The work of teachers is supported by classroom assistants and other staff. Although the two groups have distinct roles, their work is complementary. Effective team working means each member has a clear understanding of their own roles and responsibilities and those of others.

  Every school is required to have a member of staff with responsibility for co-ordinating the provision for special educational needs. Additional support may be provided for some pupils who have statements of special educational need and for pupils for whom English is an additional language. If a school has a designated support base for pupils with statements, staffing levels should reflect the guidance in DFE Circular 11/90.

  There are no statutory standards for assessing the adequacy of accommodation. DFEE bulletins give advice on space and other features. The accommodation must conform with building regulations, be safe and healthy and allow the school to provide the statutory curriculum.

  Learning resources should be appropriate in range, quality and quantity and deployed well. Some pupils may have statements of need which identify specific additional items of equipment and teaching support. Adaptations may have to be made to accommodation and furniture to meet the needs of pupils with physical or sensory disabilities.

- Overall judgements should identify the strengths of the school's staffing, accommodation and learning resources and highlight shortfalls which affect the educational standards achieved and the quality of education provided. The report should only describe aspects of a school's provision for this purpose.

USING THE CRITERIA

Do the number, qualifications and experience of teachers and other classroom staff match the demands of the curriculum?

- The staff as a whole should have sufficient knowledge and expertise to teach the National Curriculum, religious education and other aspects of the school's curriculum, including personal, social, health and careers education. In 11-18 schools the extent to which teachers have expertise appropriate to post-16 courses, including vocational courses, is an important factor.

  Inspectors should assess the extent to which the level of staffing enables the curriculum to be taught effectively to all pupils.

Guidance on using the schedule

They should also consider whether there are enough appropriately skilled support staff to enable teaching, administration and the day-to-day life of the school to function effectively, and the extent to which curriculum support staff work with teachers in planning, teaching and recording pupils' progress.

Inspectors should establish whether teaching and support staff who work with pupils with special educational needs, or with pupils for whom English is an additional language, are experienced and qualified for such work. Judgements need to be made about the appropriateness and quality of additional staffing resources, such as therapy or medical support, where provided in relation to individual statements of special educational needs.

Do arrangements for the induction, appraisal and professional development of staff contribute to their effectiveness?

■ In all schools, but particularly where there is a high staff turnover, inspectors should enquire into the adequacy of the arrangements for inducting all staff new to the school, and for those assuming new roles and responsibilities. In the case of newly qualified teachers, inspectors should establish whether the induction arrangements take account of DFEE guidance.

Procedures for teacher appraisal should be in line with national requirements. Appraisal (including the appraisal of support staff where a scheme is in place) should help staff evaluate and improve their practice. Inspectors do not have access to individual appraisal records.

Attention should also be given to the effectiveness of the staff development and in-service training programme in motivating staff and in identifying and meeting individual and corporate needs. Inspectors should look for evidence of the contribution of professional development to the quality of teaching.

Does the accommodation, including specialist accommodation and facilities for outdoor activities, allow the curriculum to be taught effectively?

■ Accommodation should be inspected in terms of its adequacy for the numbers on roll and ages of pupils as well as the range of specialist curriculum activities expected of 11-18 year olds. Coverage should include the arrangements made to use specialist accommodation off-site.

The team should come to a view about the quality of accommodation, including outdoor areas, and whether it provides a stimulating and well-maintained learning environment. Particular attention should be given to how well the accommodation, furniture and acoustics enable pupils with physical and sensory disabilities to access all areas of the curriculum.

Are learning resources adequate for the school's curriculum and range of pupils?

■ Inspectors should judge whether the level of provision, deployment and condition of books, materials and equipment held centrally and in departments enhance the quality of the work in different subjects or areas of learning, and if the range of resources is appropriate to pupils' age and needs. Good-quality resources will reflect the variety of pupils' interests and present gender and cultural diversity in a positive way.

The team should judge whether the library or learning resource centre is adequately resourced to enable it to play a central role in supporting learning. (Notes on school libraries are given at the end of this section.)

The provision of information technology resources across the curriculum, and their use to support learning, should also be assessed by the whole team. In some schools pupils will be provided with technological communication aids; their adequacy should be checked.

For vocational courses at KS4 and post-16, inspectors should consider the extent to which students have access to learning resources to support the independent learning requirements of their courses.

Most schools use resources beyond the school, including museums, galleries and field centres, to enrich the curriculum. Judgements about the effectiveness of their use will usually be based on discussion and scrutiny of work.

MAIN SOURCES OF EVIDENCE

Before the inspection

◆ the *Headteacher's Form and Statement* indicate the number and range of teachers and support staff;

◆ the **preliminary visit** will give initial impressions of staffing, accommodation and learning resources and may raise some views to be followed up later;

◆ a **staff handbook** (if available) may give useful information about the induction, appraisal and professional development of staff;

◆ **pre-inspection meetings with governors, headteacher and parents** may raise issues about staffing, accommodation and resources.

During the inspection

Further evidence includes:

◆ **Scrutiny of timetables, examination of planning documents** and discussions with the headteacher, teachers and support staff to show whether the quality of staffing is enhanced by the **deployment of teachers** to provide specialist teaching and the **deployment of support staff and visiting specialists**;

◆ **observation of lessons**;

◆ a **survey of all the available accommodation and facilities** on the school site including corridors, playing fields, environmental areas and playgrounds, and any adaptations for pupils with special educational needs. Consideration should be given to whether the provision enhances or constrains the quality of education provided. Inspectors should evaluate the impact of recent decisions taken by the school about its accommodation or resources;

◆ a **scrutiny of the library and its use**, resource collections, specialist areas, museum/art loans, to assess their impact on the breadth of the curriculum and its ability to address the needs of all pupils.

ADDITIONAL NOTES

SCHOOL LIBRARIES

Almost all secondary schools have a central library, holding fiction and non-fiction books as well as audio, video and computer resources and a range of other materials. Some schools have access to resources and services from outside the school, particularly through the schools library service. Some departments also hold specialist collections, for example, of fiction in English, source materials in history and reference books in art. The range, quality, organisation and, particularly the use made of this variety of provision need to be inspected.

Inspectors need to decide whether the accommodation in the central library is suitable and accessible for use by classes of pupils as well as by groups and individuals. The ratio of books to pupils is given on the *Headteacher's Form*. Inspectors will need to sample the range of stock to decide whether there are enough books and other resources to meet the requirements of the school's current curriculum and that they are suitable for both the age range of the pupils and their competence as readers. They will need to decide whether the resources support pupils' learning, leisure and career interests and whether they reflect and expand pupils' cultural backgrounds. Inspectors will also need to see whether the use of the library is both taught and encouraged in the context of ongoing classroom work as well as through any central 'information skills' programme. They need to observe and talk to pupils in lessons and in breaks and lunchtimes to determine the use pupils make of the resources to support their learning.

The inspection team needs to determine whether there are effective arrangements to involve subject staff in both the selection of resources and the promotion of a wide range of reading skills, and to investigate the levels of pupils' borrowing, to judge whether the library is adequately staffed so that stocks are properly organised and accessible to pupils. In summary, inspectors need to judge the library's effectiveness as a resource for personal study and its contribution in encouraging pupils to read widely and to value reading as a source of information and pleasure.

Inspection schedule

6.3 THE EFFICIENCY OF THE SCHOOL

INSPECTORS MUST EVALUATE AND REPORT ON

■ the efficiency and effectiveness with which the resources made available to the school are managed, including the use made of specific grants, and the allocation and use of funds for pupils with special educational needs[23].

■ the extent to which the school provides value for money.

Judgements should be based on the extent to which:

◆ educational developments are supported through careful financial planning;

◆ effective use is made of staff, accommodation and learning resources;

◆ there is efficient financial control and school administration;

◆ the school provides value for money in terms of the educational standards achieved and quality of education provided in relation to its context and income.

---

23 Where a school's budget is in deficit or has an undue surplus, the report should record this together with the school's reasons and, where appropriate, the measures being taken to address this matter.

INSPECTION FOCUS

■ An efficient school makes good use of all its available resources to achieve the best possible educational outcomes for all its pupils – and in doing so provides excellent value for money. This section calls for a summative judgement on the basis of the findings on all aspects of the school's work.

■ Locally-managed LEA-maintained or grant-maintained secondary schools have considerable discretion over their spending. Their governing bodies have direct responsibility for oversight of financial management: their task is to ensure that the school can account for the expenditure to which it is committed; that it budgets systematically for new expenditure; and that it regularly analyses the use of resources. Inspectors should be conversant with the differences in financial regulations and responsibilities between LEA and GM schools.

The sources of funding and patterns of expenditure in LEA-maintained schools may be complicated by the devolution (sometimes outside formal delegation) of funding for services which form discretionary elements of the Potential Schools Budget (the PSB). For all schools there may also be grant funding from GEST and other sources, such as the Single Regeneration Budget, City Challenge, European Union and Section 11 schemes.

Some LEAs have delegated all funding for special educational needs to schools; others have devolved funding for non-statemented pupils and retained funding for statemented provision; while others keep centrally all additional funding for special educational needs provision. Schools' use of this funding should be assessed.

In 11-18 schools, inspectors should analyse the post-16 funding and expenditure. Schools can deploy their resources between the main school and post-16 as they see fit, but unless there are good strategic reasons for an imbalance it would normally be reasonable to expect the expenditure on post-16 provision to be roughly the same as the proportion of the budget generated by post-16 students.

The post-16 pattern may include joint provision with other schools and/or with FEFC sector colleges. Consortium, franchising or purchasing arrangements may be used to provide vocational or minority A/AS-level courses. To maintain a viable sixth-form curriculum some courses may operate with small numbers of students. These will normally be offset by relatively large groups in other subjects. Strategies used by some schools for reducing the costs of small groups include combining AS and A-level classes, combining year groups and using supported self-study with reduced teacher contact time.

Community education provision is normally outside the scope of Section 9 inspection, although funding of it may not be easily distinguishable from that for school provision.

■ Overall judgements need to recognise that schools face financial constraints and choices. The key task is to assess the impact of the school's decisions: the way the available funding is used in relation to its educational priorities and to effect improvement. Judgements should cover the deployment of staff and the use of accommodation and learning resources. Particular attention should be given to the use of funding to meet special educational needs and the use of specific grants.

Guidance on using the schedule

Close consideration should be given to budget planning where the school has a significant surplus or a significant deficit on its current budget. The report should record the reasons given by the school for this position and the action it intends to take. In analysing any surplus inspectors should take account of committed expenditure which may not yet have been invoiced and of the school's budgeting for major expenditure in the future. Although prudent management requires contingency funding, a surplus exceeding 5% of income should be carefully evaluated. Any significant deficit needs to be viewed in the light of the school's likely budget prospects and, in the case of LEA-maintained schools, the LEA's policy on planned overspend.

Value for money can only be judged after considering all the inspection evidence about the educational standards achieved and the quality of education provided, setting this in relation to the school's context and income. In PRUs, inspectors should take into account the success with which pupils are re-integrated into schools.

USING THE CRITERIA

Are educational developments supported through careful financial planning?

■ Evaluation against this criterion needs to be seen in relation to Sections 6.1 and 6.2.

Inspectors should review the funding available to the school in the previous and current year through the delegated local management formula budget share or the annual maintenance grant, together with any further devolved funding, including funding for pupils with special educational needs, specific grants and other income.

Inspectors should examine the use of the funding for different purposes, including provision for teaching staff, support staff, curriculum development, learning resources and premises. Some comparison of the costs per pupil and the percentage of income spent on different items can be derived from the PICSI, which gives information on the range and median levels of expenditure. These need to be interpreted in the school context. Comparison must be tentative because of the differences between LMS schemes throughout the country and because of differences in other income. The circumstances of schools also differ, particularly in relation to staffing and premises costs. They may also be affected by factors outside schools' control – most obviously changes in LEA spending and in pupil numbers.

An effective process of school development planning will focus on improving educational outcomes and relate expenditure to this. Even where the room for manoeuvre on the use of funding is marginal, the school should be able to demonstrate that it budgets systematically for new and well-focused expenditure, for example on learning resources, rather than relying on previous patterns – but minute detail should not be expected. Inspectors should look for evidence that the school plans ahead. Depending on when the inspection falls it would be reasonable to expect detailed planning to be under way for the forthcoming year, with outline planning for at least one or two years beyond.

Inspectors should consider how the governing body is fulfilling its strategic responsibility for planning the use of resources. The key to the judgement will be whether financial planning is based on good current data and sound projections, whether consideration has been given to alternative strategies for managing expenditure and for handling contingencies, and whether the school is clear about priorities. Inspectors should also assess the extent to which staff with management responsibility are involved in or informed about financial planning.

Is effective use made of staff, accommodation and learning resources?

■ Inspectors need to draw on the inspection evidence, especially the evidence from subject inspection, to determine how well the resources of staff, accommodation and learning resources are used. Both provision and use can be a guide to the quality of planning in the past.

Particular attention should be given to :

◆ the efficiency of the school's staffing arrangements, taking into account curriculum organisation, class size and contact time;

◆ the deployment of additional teaching and support staff for pupils with special educational needs and those for whom English is an additional language, including any staff financed through specific grants.

Is there efficient financial control and school administration?

■ Detailed advice on financial administration is given in *Keeping Your Balance: Standards for Financial Administration in Schools*. Schools are asked to complete the financial questionnaire which is part of the *Headteacher's Statement*.

Inspectors should establish whether the main recommendations in the latest audit report available to the school have been acted on. They are not expected to undertake a detailed check on the school's financial procedures themselves and should not become preoccupied with them. The judgement should focus on whether financial administration is sound and carried out with a minimum of management time so that adequate information is available to the headteacher and governors and finances are kept in good order.

Secondary schools are likely to have computerised financial management systems which allow for modelling of expenditure projections and provide sophisticated accounting. Not all schools have or need such systems with which to control a budget with a high level of committed expenditure and limited flexibility.

Inspectors should evaluate the school's administrative procedures. At best, they should be unobtrusive, resulting in efficient day-to-day organisation and the capacity to respond to the unforeseen event. Administration is at its best where it gives clear support to the central purposes of the school, keeping the way clear for teachers to focus on their work with pupils and supporting their endeavours.

Guidance on using the schedule

Does the school provide value for money in terms of educational standards achieved and quality of education provided in relation to its context and income?

■ The value for money afforded by the school is a summative judgement which relates the educational standards achieved and the quality of education provided by a school to its income, taking account of any appropriate contextual factors and using comparison with similar schools as available. Some schools may have higher than average costs, but their achievement may be significantly higher than similar schools or their costs may be high owing to factors outside the school's control.

Judgements should be based on the team's conclusions about:

◆ pupils' attainment and progress, attitudes to learning, behaviour, personal development and attendance;

◆ the quality of education provided and the effectiveness with which staffing, accommodation and learning resources are used;

◆ the cost-effectiveness of major spending decisions;

◆ in PRUs, the rate of re-integration into school.

The table opposite may be useful in ordering judgements.

EVALUATING VALUE FOR MONEY

The table uses key judgement recording statements. A school giving the very best value for money would have judgements on contextual factors coded as 7 and judgements on outcomes, provision and expenditure coded as 1, and average unit costs.

Judgement recording grade		1	2	3	4	5	6	7	
CONTEXTUAL FACTORS									
The socio-economic circumstances of pupils are:	Very favourable	*	*	*	*	*	*		Very unfavourable
The attainment of the intake on entry is:	Very high	*	*	*	*	*	*	*	Very low
OUTCOMES									
Pupils' attainment in relation to national averages or expectations is:	Excellent	*	*	*	*	*	*	*	Very poor
Pupils' progress is:	Excellent	*	*	*	*	*	*	*	Very poor
The attitudes, behaviour and personal development of pupils at the school are:	Excellent	*	*	*	*	*	*	*	Very poor
PROVISION									
The quality of education, particularly teaching, provided by the school is:	Excellent	*	*	*	*	*	*	*	Very poor
EXPENDITURE									
Unit cost for a school of this type is:	Very low	*	*	*	*	*	*	*	Very high
VALUE FOR MONEY JUDGEMENT									
The value for money provided by the school is:	Excellent	*	*	*	*	*	*	*	Very poor

Guidance on using the schedule

MAIN SOURCES OF EVIDENCE

Before the inspection

◆ the PICSI report, *Headteacher's Form* and *Statement* will provide the context for forming preliminary views on efficiency;

◆ **school documentation on financial planning and administration**, budgetary information, including out-turn statements, and copies of auditors' reports will all provide important background information;

◆ **the school development plan** should indicate whether the school has set clear objectives for the main tasks it faces, has identified the resources needed to achieve them, and evaluated its work and spending including any analysis of cost-effectiveness;

◆ **minutes of governing body meetings** will help to determine the governors' role in maintaining the efficiency of the school;

◆ **pre-inspection meetings** with governors, the headteacher and parents are opportunities to explore some of the issues emerging from a reading of the documentation.

During the inspection

◆ **discussion** with governors, headteacher, bursar or clerical officer, and staff, particularly those with financial responsibilities, should help to determine how major budgetary, staffing or resource decisions were taken, how they were implemented and with what effect. This will provide evidence of the decision-making process in action;

◆ **general observation** of lessons and school routines will provide evidence of the impact on the quality of education of decisions made about the management of resources.

PART B: CURRICULUM AREAS AND SUBJECTS

Note: Section 7 of the Framework does not apply to the inspection of secondary schools.

8 English, mathematics and science

FOR EACH SUBJECT THE REPORT MUST INCLUDE EVALUATION OF

- pupils' attainment in relation to national expectations or standards, drawing on evidence of what pupils know, understand and can do by the end of the relevant stage;

- progress made in relation to pupils' prior attainment;

- pupils' attitudes to learning; and

- any strengths and weaknesses in teaching and other factors which contribute to the standards achieved in the subject.

In English, the subject report up to 16 should also draw on evidence of contributions made by other subjects to pupils' competence in reading, writing, speaking and listening. In mathematics, the report should draw on evidence of the use of number in other subjects.

9 Other subjects and courses

FOR EACH SUBJECT OR COURSE INSPECTED, THE REPORT MUST INCLUDE EVALUATION OF

- each of the aspects indicated above where there is sufficient evidence.

In this section, subjects may be grouped or reported on separately, as is appropriate to the size of the school, the way it organises teaching, and the extent of the evidence available.

In information technology, the report should draw on evidence from all the other subjects inspected.

Guidance on using the schedule

INSPECTION FOCUS

- The inspection of subjects and courses of the curriculum should focus on pupils' attainment and progress; teaching and other aspects of provision which make a significant contribution to what is achieved; and pupils' response.

- In **schools other than PRUs**, National Curriculum subjects, together with religious education[24] and any provision specified in the contract, must be inspected and reported upon. In PRUs, all subjects offered should be covered.

In **secondary schools,** the organisation of the curriculum is mainly subject-based although there may in addition be personal and social education courses and vocational courses at KS4. It is important that, whatever the form of organisation, the attainment and progress and the quality of provision, particularly teaching, in subjects of the National Curriculum are evaluated and reported upon.

In secondary schools a separate report should be written on each subject in all but exceptional circumstances. In the cases where subjects are grouped, a clear evaluation of each subject must be included.

Inspection of National Curriculum subjects must be based on knowledge and understanding by inspectors of the National Curriculum subject Orders. Inspection of non-denominational RE will be in relation to the relevant agreed syllabus, and inspectors need to have knowledge of this. Inspectors also need to be familiar with the requirements of GCSE and other relevant qualifications.

Post-16 provision may include A/AS-level, GNVQ or NVQ courses, as well as GCSE and other courses. Inspection must be based on knowledge and understanding by inspectors of the nature and requirements of these courses.

Before the inspection inspectors should be able to form a view of attainment and progress from public examination and other accredited course results at 16 and 18 years. At KS3, National Curriculum teacher assessment and test results will be available in English, mathematics and science. Analysis of attainment data, taking account of any analyses carried out by the school, is a key pre-inspection task. Documentation available before inspection may indicate the extent to which the school's planning is in line with National Curriculum requirements. Any apparent failure to comply with statutory requirements should be pursued during the inspection.

During the inspection the major source of evidence will be work in the classroom, although teachers' records, assessment results, displayed work, portfolios, reports, and discussions with teachers and pupils all play their part. While the school is in session, inspectors should focus on the teaching and learning actually taking place. Advice on classroom observation, talking with pupils and scrutiny of their work as sources of evidence is included in other sections of the guidance.

---

24 The 1992 Act as amended by Section 259 of the 1993 Act makes separate provision for the inspection of denominational religious education in those schools where it is provided; such inspection falls under Section 13 of the 1992 Act.

Guidance on using the schedule

Evidence relating to individual subjects will invariably be co-ordinated by one inspector, but it is likely that other inspectors will also see work in the subject, for example where inspection includes the tracking of pupils. Systems to bring together evidence on subjects need to be part of the management of the inspection.

In relation to the inspection schedule, inspectors should concentrate in particular on the following aspects:

4.1 Attainment and progress

The focus should be on attainment and progress in the subject. The criteria appropriate to the age range should be applied, and reporting should include comment on any unusual variations in attainment and progress for different groups of pupils.

4.2 Attitudes, behaviour and personal development

All the criteria should be applied. Judgements will be made in each lesson or session and in relation to the subject as a whole.

5.1 Teaching

This is a key aspect of provision on which a judgement in each subject and at each key stage is needed. All criteria should be applied, and overall judgements for the subject drawn from observations in individual lessons or sessions.

The subject report should only include reference to the other aspects of the schedule if there are particular strengths or weaknesses:

Inspectors must be fully conversant with the National Curriculum requirements for the subjects they inspect, and the contents of any guidance issued by OFSTED or the School Curriculum and Assessment Authority on the inspection, teaching or assessment of those subjects.

Inspection schedule

PART C: INSPECTION DATA

10 Summary of inspection evidence

THE REPORT MUST INCLUDE

a concise, factual statement summarising the number of inspectors; the number of inspector days spent gathering first-hand evidence; the total time spent in classes, discussion with pupils and evaluation of their work; and a brief comment about other evidence.

It may be appropriate to refer to the timing of the inspection and any interruption in the normal programme of the school. Where a subject is not being taught at the time of the inspection, or where other exceptional circumstances reduce the coverage of inspection, the report should state this clearly.

11 Data and indicators

THE REPORT MUST INCLUDE

PUPILS

Number of pupils on roll

Number of pupils having a statement of special educational needs

Number of pupils on the special educational needs register

Number of full-time pupils eligible for free school meals

TEACHERS AND CLASSES

Number of qualified teachers (full-time equivalent)

Number of pupils per qualified teacher

Average class size (primary and nursery schools)

Average teaching group size by key stage (secondary and special schools)

Percentage of time teachers spend in contact with classes (secondary schools)

FINANCIAL DATA

Summary balance sheet, including expenditure per pupil, for the latest available financial year

PARENTAL SURVEY

A summary of the responses to the parents' questionnaire (when issued)

Guidance on using the schedule

PARENTS' QUESTIONNAIRE

Registered inspectors are required to report the results of the parents' questionnaire, when it has been used, in section 11 of the report of the inspection. It will also be included in the summary of the report.

All reporting of the questionnaire must include the number of questionnaires sent out, the number returned and the percentage return rate.

In most cases the report should include a table setting out, for each question, the percentage of ticks in each column. There should also be a short commentary on any other issues raised by parents on the forms.

Registered inspectors must exercise particular care in reporting the results of the questionnaire when numbers of returns are small. Small numbers of returns are unlikely to be statistically significant and should not be used as the basis for generalisations. There is also a potential problem with the confidentiality of the responses. In a very small school, or where the response has been small, it may be possible to identify individual responses from a detailed breakdown.

Where there are small numbers of returned questionnaires a short verbal summary of the responses will suffice.

It is difficult to be precise about the numbers involved, and registered inspectors will need to use their judgement about the circumstances of each school, but usually **a minimum of 20 returned questionnaires are needed.**

INDEX

Printed in the United Kingdom for HMSO
Dd 301988 C30 1/96